WHEN WISHES CHANGE

What if the thing you feared most brings more than you dreamed?

TRICIA ROOS

WESTBOW
P R E S S®
A DIVISION OF THOMAS NELSON
& ZONDERVAN

WestBow Press books may be ordered through booksellers or by contacting:

WestBow Press
A Division of Thomas Nelson & Zondervan
1663 Liberty Drive
Bloomington, IN 47403
www.westbowpress.com
844-714-3454

Scriptures taken from the Holy Bible, New International Version®, NIV®. Copyright © 1973, 1978, 1984, 2011 by Biblica, Inc.™ Used by permission of Zondervan. All rights reserved worldwide. www.zondervan.com The "NIV" and "New International Version" are trademarks registered in the United States Patent and Trademark Office by Biblica, Inc.®

ISBN: 978-1-6642-4216-6 (sc)
ISBN: 978-1-6642-4218-0 (hc)
ISBN: 978-1-6642-4217-3 (e)

Library of Congress Control Number: 2021915865

Print information available on the last page.

WestBow Press rev. date: 08/26/2021

To our darling Annabelle,
more than we ever wished for

"This isn't a mistake. There's a higher purpose to this."
Tricia Roos, Dallas Morning News, Sept. 23, 2014

CONTENTS

Introduction xi

Part One: What You Wish For
Chapter 1   Lady Baby 1
Chapter 2   Jonas 4
Chapter 3   Bebis 7
Chapter 4   Heartbeat 11
Chapter 5   Kanga 15
Chapter 6   Testing 17
Chapter 7   Getting Home 20
Chapter 8   Oceans 23
Chapter 9   Deeper 27
Chapter 10 Email 30
Chapter 11 Grace 36
Chapter 12 Water 40
Chapter 13 Vision 43
Chapter 14 Undefeated 50
Chapter 15 Lies 59
Chapter 16 State 62
Chapter 17 Reality 70
Chapter 18 Christmas 75

Part Two: A Wish in Time
Day One 83
Day Two 89
Day Three 93
Day Four 98
Day Five 104
Day Six 107
Day Seven 111
Day Eight 116
A Dream Come True 120

Part Three: Wish Again
Every Ending is a Beginning 127

Acknowledgements 135

INTRODUCTION

It was more than coincidence. I had told my husband I knew I was supposed to write our daughter's story, and maybe a day later one of those cookies-in-your-brain ads showed up on my Facebook page: *Need to write your novel? Take this class!* The site touted author and teacher Mary Adkins. My forehead scrunched: *How do I know that name?* The picture by the name was of one of my best friends' sisters, and what are the chances? I called Katie Beth and, sure enough, she put me in touch with her sister Mary. And the course was so life-changing that this paragraph is a product placement.

Fast forward a year. My first draft was written. After a two-month hiatus, I began to edit . . . and it turns out I'm no editor. Pouring my story onto paper had given me energy. Trying to polish it made me want to head out for a run and never stop running.

One rainy Sunday afternoon in January, I waved a white flag. "I have no aptitude for this," I said to God. I shut my laptop and closed my mind. Two minutes later, with my computer still on my legs and evidently not all the way shut, I heard the *bing* of an incoming email. It was a note from Laura Pfeil—a science teacher from school, by no means a close friend or anyone I talk with often.

Hi Tricia, she wrote. *I'm thinking about you and your daughter Annabelle, and how you loved her during the time she was with you. I recall that doctors discouraged you from continuing the pregnancy, but a lot of people are better because you took the hard road. I pray for many, many blessings to you and your family.* – Laura

This interruption in my self-pity, timed even better than the Facebook ad, had me wiping tears before I laughed out loud. Does God lead us? In the Bible he speaks to us, I know that. In my daily life, he whispers and points in impressions and events that come between long stretches of not knowing. His nudges are more than coincidence, less than an email or text, and what I choose to do with them calls for faith, prayer and courage.

Okay, God, I said looking up from the email, I'm listening for real about this book thing. Editing outstripped my skills, but Annabelle's life outsized her days, and if her story had a place in God's story, I trusted him to help me get it told.

A month or two after Laura's email, still struggling with book details but certain that a lot of intel is a podcast, a google search, or a conversation away, I made a phone call. I'd just read another piece by Peggy Wehmeyer, mother of two of my childhood friends. When her daughters and I were kids living across a creek from each other, Peggy was the religion reporter for ABC World News Tonight. Now her essays ran in the Wall Street Journal, New York Times, Dallas Morning News, and I read every one. She draws on her life to show how faith factors in the real world, and that speaks to me. Just as important, her writing stands up and walks off the page, which I wanted for Annabelle's story.

Peggy thanked me for the compliments and shared the credit with Nancy Lovell, her editor and longtime friend. "Nancy makes it sparkle," she said, and I thought, *sparkle: good verb*, and in a moment similar to the Facebook ad and the email, I knew who I wanted to edit.

By the end of my first lunch with Nancy, I also knew what to name the book. It's more than a story, I was telling her. It's like a travelogue through a hard time with scenes people relate to, and human nature . . . and humor. My readers are saying they laugh and cry and get a new picture of God's love—and that's the point.

In our common love for Annabelle, God changed what I knew of trust, marriage, faith, perseverance, overcoming, sports, community, obedience, humility, mystery . . . Because of the child who rewrote the book on a rare condition, a day came when, still grieving her death, I could also praise God for it. I'm not sure of all I told Nancy that day over tacos for me and tuna salad for her, but she jotted something on a notepad with her. When I paused, she said, "That phrase you used, 'when wishes change.'"

When Wishes Change is an endurance love story, a mother's version of scaling Mt. Everest, an account of how I got to my child, and the handles that grew out of sheer rock once I committed to the climb. Annabelle's birth and death are an open-eyed look at sometimes blind trust, and it matters to tell it because trust is the lesson we humans keep having to learn.

Recently, during some unexpected changes in my life, I confided to a friend that I felt ignored and devalued. I was doubting myself. Even as I wrote about the trust I'd gained through Annabelle, I was having to submit my knee-jerk anger and hurt, my wishes, *again*, to God's sovereignty. As Joseph learned when he was sold by his brothers and betrayed by Potiphar's wife, I was relearning that whatever happens, for whatever reasons, God means it for good.

That alone may be the message of *When Wishes Change*: God means it for good. When the only school on your list turns you down, when your boss lets you go or the coach passes you by, when your fiancé meets someone else or there's no fiancé at all, when a tumor is malignant or a parent dies . . . when a remark wounds, a friend pulls back, a bank account evaporates, a setback lands, the world crashes into pieces . . . your story has more to go. God is involved, loving you, working in the pain to give you more than you could have dreamed.

When Wishes Change is my path from "God, please, please, please" to "not my will but thine." Part I, *What You Wish For*, goes from expecting the world, to straining just to finish the day. Part II, *A Wish in Time*, breaks into days and hours—sometimes moments—the kind of perseverance that hurts the most and leaves the fewest regrets. Part III, *Wish Again,* is the far side of trusting God with my longings. The Bible speaks of the treasures of darkness. As God continues to turn up the light on my darkest hours, I can see what some of those treasures are.

Short version: This book is my story and your truth. We have desires, we have hard times. When the two collide and everything changes, the good news is that God does not change, and that we can.

One

WHAT YOU WISH FOR

CHAPTER 1

LADY BABY

———————————

"**M**OMMY, I WANT a lady baby." My blue-eyed toddler was placing an order from the backseat.

"A what?"

"A lady baby."

By definition parents of toddlers are bilingual, and as a rule I could keep up with my son's logic. "Cameron," I said, only glancing into the rearview because I also intended to stay on the highway, "what is a lady baby? And why do you think you need one?"

"TJ got a lady baby," he said, and there it was. Context. Cameron's buddy at daycare had a sister named Addie, a pudgy little princess, and Cameron believed we could use one. Addie was probably eighteen months old, but she had just moved into the daycare classroom next door, and Cameron was processing available data.

Maybe he was thinking of a lady baby pickup on the way home. We could swing by a shop with miscellaneous newborns, insist on a cute one, and toss in the starter accessories. It also struck me that our conversation had quickly entered uncharted waters. So far, no parenting blog I'd read had laid out the birds-and-bees talk for toddlers.

"Cameron, you pray for a lady baby, and maybe God will send us one," I said, improvising. Prayer and God should occupy him like a piece of candy in each hand. In the rearview, I saw a pale round face register a conclusion.

"Mommy, can I have a snack?"

We pulled into our driveway in East Dallas, and I set up Cameron with LEGO bricks in the living room while I straightened up before my husband, Jonas, got home. This boy was an only child and livin' the dream: his toys to himself, an iPad, minimal competition for the remote. The lady baby he was so sure he wanted would upend far more than he knew to brace for. As it happened, I wanted one too. But life was busy, and Jonas and I so far weren't on the same page about it.

> Prayer and God should occupy him like a piece of candy in each hand.

My sister, three years younger than me, was my childhood companion, my competition for outfits as we grew up, and when we grew up all the way, my best friend for life. We played endless hours of Barbie in our closets and snuck into each other's rooms at night for shadow-puppet shows. When our parents' divorce uprooted us from Dallas to a small-town Texas high school, we had each other. A good sibling is the gift that never ends, and I wanted that for Cameron.

Jonas got home and started dinner. He and I caught up in the kitchen while Cameron migrated to Mickey Mouse Clubhouse. My husband is a financial planner, meaning besides an emotional appeal, another baby would have to make financial sense.

"Cameron asked me something funny today," I said, pulling a grape off a stem. I watched Jonas lay a burger in the skillet.

"What about?"

"He said he would like a lady baby!" I said with a laugh.

"A what?"

"I had the same reaction. I figured out he wants us to have another baby, and he wants it to be a girl because that's what TJ has."

Silence spread like olive oil on the kitchen counter. Jonas said, "You think we're ready? With our jobs and everything we have going on?"

"I think we are," I said. "By the time I get pregnant and have the baby, the kids would be about four years apart."

This was mid-February. Cameron's birthday was in April. A winter or early spring baby would be good timing, but that was the planner in me. Jonas studied the burgers, and then he half turned my direction and said okay.

Okay? Okay. *Okay* was good. I would take *okay*.

A voice shouted from the living room. "Mommy, I need you!" Back to full-on Cameron coverage. If another child joined us in the next year, this one should get it while he could.

CHAPTER 2

JONAS

THE RUSH OF spring activity hurtled the Roos family toward May, when school ended and a long-planned trip to Sweden filled the horizon. Jonas was sixteen years old when Ericsson Telecom had transplanted his father's work and family from Stockholm to Plano. The rest of his family—no small group—was still in Sweden and overdue to meet the first grandchild, a miniature Jonas growing by the day.

Packing us all for ten days overseas was doable for me. Leaving our house in a semblance of order was in the realm of possibility. The challenge to our trip, as I saw it, was getting an active little boy through an eighteen-hour flight with the least input from air marshals or sleep-deprived adults.

By the morning of the flight, amid washing underwear and dividing crackers into Ziploc bags, it made sense to take a pregnancy test. The kitchen conference with Jonas in February had greenlighted our trying again. This was month three, when it's possible to know something, and I rummaged through bathroom drawers.

Every woman who has ever taken a home pregnancy test knows

the moments when time stands still. *If it's positive, what then? If it's negative, will I cry? What's the due date?* And in my case: *Will I get sick on the trip, and did I pack toothpaste?* One minute. Two. Three, four . . . a peek couldn't hurt. My chest pounded like sneakers in a dryer. *Please, Lord, let it be positive. Let it be positive.* A quarter hour before, my goal in life had been to find the Spider-Man pajama top. Deep breath. Peek.

Positive.

Jonas was in the shower thinking I was busy packing. In a movie, this scene would cut to a soft-focus pregnancy reveal. Flowers. Candlelight. She's in a flowing red dress. Over dessert, she slips a note onto his plate.

"Jonas!" I screamed as he stepped from the shower, a towel around his waist. "I'm pregnant!!" Dripping puddles, hair plastered on his head, my husband froze and we locked stares. Then one of us moved, and the tears, jumping, hugs and kisses began until someone had the good sense to look at the clock. The test and the results would be our secret. When we came back, we'd tell friends and family.

———

Two types of travelers take long flights: those who tolerate small children and those who see small children on board and scan for an option to parachute out. In the terminal around us, faces showed either big smiles and looks of delight or undisguised disgust, and I was the mother of the controversy. As we walked down the aisle of the plane, a few older women cooed at Cameron's little round face. Most of our fellow passengers showed relief to see us move along.

I wanted to press small notes into the hands of every person onboard. "No parents of young children dream of taking them to Europe," the note would say. "We dream about babysitters." This was a business trip, a family appearance, and that should be in the note too.

The plane's seats ran eleven across: three on the right, five in the middle, another three on the left. I hoped for a three-across section, but our seats were smack in the middle, next to a large man who, all by himself, owned the category of travelers who disapprove of small children on long flights. An audible sigh escaped me. Buckling in, I prayed for patience for me, grace for our fellow passengers, and endless naps for Cameron.

Thank God for headphones and TV screens on the backs of airplane seats. Thank God for children's entertainment. Cameron settled into unlimited cartoons and snacks on demand. Were we in heaven? I wrapped an arm around my son's thin shoulders, his mouth crunching animal crackers, his eyes glued to *Wreck-It Ralph*, and I knew it was too good to last.

But it did last, and all the way to Sweden. True, Cameron never slept. But the adults around us did, including the chair of the International Alliance against Underage Travelers. Did Cameron stay in his seat? Let me ask you: Barring bathroom breaks, what child would leave endless candy and TV? What I learned about taking my three-year-old to Sweden was that his mother needed to chill, and that my son's catching up on every episode of *Paw Patrol* and my husband with a biography was my time to think. No, even more than *think*, it was my time for wonder.

How quickly, how profoundly, a family's world can change. During the flight, the joy of my pregnancy swelled to dwarf every other thought. In hours, our new baby had become a part of my being. Any physical turbulence ahead was a small price for our new son or daughter.

What I couldn't know, could in no way anticipate, were the anomalies in the child in my womb and in my pregnancy, and where they would take us. But those things were in the future. For now, we were in the clouds.

CHAPTER 3

BEBIS

———

N O TRAVEL BROCHURE, webpage or Instagram story can do justice to Sweden. If you go there in May, multiply that by ten. Daytime temperatures waft into the mid-sixties; evenings dip into "bracing but humane." In the balance is relief from the heat of a Dallas summer, which no self-respecting travel writer would try to romance.

For the Roos of Dallas, the weather in Sweden could be topped only by our one-woman welcome committee—Mormor, Jonas's mother's mother—whose superpower is making her loved ones feel like royalty. Two bedraggled American parents and a restless three-year-old landed at Stockholm Arlanda Airport, lumbered into the luggage-carousel area, and there she was, small and gray-haired, in sensible shoes . . . squeezing, exclaiming, chatting away in her best attempts at English, wrapping us in spring with every Swedish-saturated syllable.

Pre-Cameron, the only other time Jonas and I had come here, we'd booked our trip for our days off at work, which overlapped, regrettably, with Mormor's trip to see her sister. But in the three days she was in Danderyd and we were in her house, Mormor raised the bar on thoughtfulness in absentia. In every room we found notes typed and taped on cupboards and walls. "Use this bath mat so you don't slip and fall in the shower." "These are the cups to drink your coffee."

Mormor lives twenty miles north of Stockholm in a hamlet called Sollentuna, where Jonas grew up with his parents and all four of his grandparents. In the fifteen years since his family had moved to Texas, Jonas told me, not a chair had changed. But why mess with paradise? Every house or cottage spilled with blooms in the flower beds and children in the yards. Every sidewalk and pathway crowded with Swedes, committed walkers all, resulting in highways that in America would seem half empty.

Driving into Sollentuna, our car slowed at the roundabouts and rolled into Mormor's picturesque swath of streets, and we felt our blood pressures drop. Dallas lawns sprawl from big houses to wide sidewalks, but here at each tidy home a gate opens to a fenced-in garden—another building block of Swedish life. On the cobblestone walk to Mormor's house, every plot outshone the last with vegetables and flowers. Every front entrance appeared to be framed in lingonberry plants with their red-pearl clusters.

Mormor reached her cottage door and fumbled for her keys. Turning to us, then, with a Vanna White flourish, she declared in English, "Welcome to my home! I am so happy that you are here!" Cameron darted past her like a puppy, circling the kitchen and living space, bounding upstairs to the bedrooms and bathroom. "This is so cool!" an all-boy voice shouted down to us. "There are toys everywhere!" Next time, I thought, we'd cross that threshold with our new baby.

———

That first day in Sweden brought my first wave of sickness. Not morning or night sickness but some all-day version, and it surprised me. So far, my pregnancy timeline was at full speed: Day One: test positive. Day Two: arrive halfway around the globe. Day Three: nausea at every smell, odor, fragrance or thought of food. Is it really that quick, I thought, the sickness? Or the second that I know that I'm pregnant, does my mind play with me?

Accepting nausea as my new normal, I tried to sightsee, to rise to family drop-ins, and to share emotional space with piles of meatballs, boiled potatoes, and sugared desserts. Every celebration of our arrival also brought out my two beverages of last choice. *Tricia, a glass of wine! Tricia, coffee!* This early in my pregnancy was too soon to explain why I wasn't eating but turning down choice vintages brought looks of dismay. Jonas and I agreed that before we left, we'd pull aside his grandmothers and spill the beans. The timing was on the early side but seeing for ourselves the joy on their faces would be worth the entire trip.

Cue a whole new set of emotions. Word of our baby was about to fly beyond "just us," and in a language I couldn't speak. On our final day in Sweden, Farmor (Jonas's father's mother) came to Mormor's house for afternoon coffee, still making me seasick. Farmor was widowed too and the two women were close, despite their children, Jonas's parents, having divorced on the other side of the world.

Dinner ended and Jonas moved us into the living room, where Cameron lost himself in a LEGO castle. The grandmothers found armchairs, and I planted myself next to my husband. Throughout our visit here, almost every conversation was in Swedish, meaning someone else had to say what I meant. This time I was eager to take part in the telling, but how? It was too late to start building a pregnancy vocabulary in another language. Maybe while Jonas spoke, I could mimic holding a baby in my arms.

In the end, what I could do was guess at his words and join in the joy. From the moment my husband cleared his throat, his grandmothers happily gave him their full attention. Next to him on a small couch, I fixed on them. Eyes wide, hands clasped, they leaned in. And then Jonas must have said "bebis"—baby—because two elderly faces began to radiate light, and never have I emoted so deeply in words I didn't understand. In seconds, we were all standing, crying, hugging, mixing exclamations in any language handy, and the newest Roos was official.

At some point, Mormor turned to me with tears. "I hope that we will find out that this baby is a girl," she said. "Me, too!" I said, thinking of Cameron's lady baby.

This time our return home was to a rich new chapter. For the entire flight, Cameron stayed in his seat, wide awake, a happy clam with movies and snacks. As the wheels of the plane touched down, he passed out and became dead weight, impervious to the crowds and noise as we took turns lugging him through customs. His new little brother or sister would join us just after New Year's. Our family time abroad had renewed my spirits to conquer work and anything else in my path.

CHAPTER 4

HEARTBEAT

———

D ALLAS SUMMERS ARE character builders. In January, February and March, my home city has bragging rights to the weather. May through September, and into October if we're honest, Dallas is a reason to see other parts of the world. In May, the heat and the humidity start at a low boil; by August, anyone who can afford it is emailing from a state with mountains. I wouldn't have voted to begin my pregnancy in May, but it would take more than Texas temperatures to throw shade on our joy.

Our first doctor's appointment in that first week of June would introduce us by sonogram to our currently bean-sized baby, and to our new doctor. The OBGYN who delivered Cameron had traded her practice for more time with her own children, and handed my file to Dr. Amy Martin, whose online reviews were five-star. (I'd checked.)

In a woman's pregnancy, the OBGYN's office is home away from home, especially toward the end, when she all but takes her mail there. Though by that time, to vastly understate, the appointments have lost their luster. But all that was later. To start this leg of the journey to expand our family, Jonas and I got into our places early.

It was four years since I'd first come to this waiting room when I was pregnant with Cameron. All the players were still there: armchairs holding mothers-in-progress, a few dads looking out of place . . . to the right of the check-in window a tank of exotic fish entertained its fan base of big brothers and sisters. Outside, the midcentury modern building might show the passage of time, but in this familiar space, the world was a constant.

I signed in and found a seat near a spread of magazines with curled edges, reading I typically avoided. That day, though, feeling new again and uncertain, I opened a *Dallas Child* and gave in to my fascination with water births, in the sense that anyone would want to have

> "Jonas and I lost ourselves in this first look at our new little one."

one. Jonas appeared in the doorway and took a seat next to me, now one of the earnest dads. In a few minutes a voice called Roos.

Up we stood and down we walked, following a worn narrow stairway to our basement exam room, small and windowless. This space I also knew: the chair and stirrups, the machine, the large screen across the room to show sonogram images. A small blonde woman in her mid-fifties came in. "Howdy, I'm Janet," she said, her voice full of West Texas. "How far along do you think you are?"

"Seven to eight weeks," I told her. She jotted on her clipboard and then pulled over a swivel chair. "Let's find out," she said. "Sit down and put up your feet."

One memory that had mercifully slipped my mind was this first sonogram. When the pregnancy is new, the exam is vaginal and singularly ungraceful. Like most of the indignities of this period, it also pales next to the rewards. Almost as soon as I took position—a description I'll spare the reader—the screen showed a blurry black-and-white image of my uterus, a large dark circle with a head and body in it, like two connected peas bouncing in a cavern.

With the skill of a thousand sonograms, Janet measured everything measurable, studied the screen, and clacked her keyboard. Jonas and I lost ourselves in this first look at our new little one.

"Want to hear the heartbeat?" Janet said after a while, and in my mind, as I too often do, I defaulted to sarcasm. *Is that a real question?*

"I do," I said, and in seconds our small room filled with the rapid staccato of a beginner's heartbeat. At six or seven weeks, a baby's pulse averages 150 beats per minute. Here was our first milestone, and from deep inside me came a long, slow exhale. In her black glasses, head tilted, our technician kept her eyes on the screen. "Everything looks great, Mama," she said.

Next stop was a windowless patient room to meet with our new doctor. In my hands I held a reel of printed images of the tiny new bundle inside me. While we waited, Jonas and I studied the hieroglyphics of my sonogram, indecipherable to anyone but doctors and parents. A door opened and a woman in a lab coat breezed in. Right away, her bright blue eyes and shoulder-length brown hair earned two checks on my short list of criteria: old enough to be experienced, young enough to relate to my stage in life. The bonus was her spirit. Shaking Dr. Martin's hand and feeling her smile was like finding a new energy source.

For twenty minutes Jonas and I reviewed sonogram results with Dr. Martin—her answering our questions as if she hadn't answered the same questions a dozen times already that day. A good amount of what a mother knows about pregnancy seems to disappear between births, God's way of helping her do it again, I think, and we were back on the learning curve. Our next appointment would be in four weeks for another sonogram and checkup. Until the birth this was our routine.

"Did the technician review your due date?" Dr. Martin said.

"No, but can you tell us what you think?"

Our pregnancy Sherpa reached into her lab-coat pocket,

produced a round laminated predictor, and rotated the wheel to 40 weeks. "January 5 or so," she said.

Perfection. The new year would deliver a package guaranteed to keep us awake nights and sleepless by day. Sign me up. Before heading back to work, Jonas and I headed for a celebratory lunch.

CHAPTER 5

KANGA

————————————————

I COULD SAY THE four weeks until my next doctor's visit flew on the wings of impending motherhood, but in my world, every year and every season speeds by. As director of admissions and head volleyball coach of the largest coed Catholic high school in Texas, I live by the school calendar, a foot in the present, a foot in the months barrelling at us. Within that rhythm, June is a banner month because it is, as families with teen volleyball players know, the unofficial start of the season.

This year our season opened on two back-to-back state championships, making our lofty aim a three-peat, and the possibilities began now, with our fall candidates. Few things make my heart race like the first meeting with our players and the incoming freshman. On top of that, I planned to announce my pregnancy. Call me biased, but there's something wonderful about giving good news to teenage girls who act as if they've won the lottery every time they see their best friend.

On June 1, after warmups and stretches, I gathered the eighty girls in a midcourt huddle, scanned the circle of hopeful faces, and to my surprise felt my spirits sag. Was this the right time?

"Hello ladies!" I shouted over the fear. "Have a seat and we'll take care of a few housekeeping items." Housekeeping is such an unlikely sports term. "I'm excited to welcome you to our first open gym. Today is about meeting new friends and working hard, so look around," I said. "Introduce yourself to people you don't know." A chorus line of ponytails and smiles swiveled right and left.

I introduced the volleyball coaching staff members, each of whom spoke briefly to the nervous girls whose fates they held. Last up was my varsity assistant, Josh Kreuter, my coaching partner of six years and three state championships, and my co-pilot in the admissions office. Josh is a leader known for his genuine concern and for bringing out the best in everyone he works with. He addressed the crowd with his scruffy beard and signature smile.

"Hey ladies, I'm excited to be coaching again this year," he said. "Let's have fun today. No pressure, just fun!" And this was my cue.

"I'm also excited to start the 2014 season at Bishop Lynch," I said. "I'm ready to work with all our freshmen as well as returning players. This year, we again defend our state championship, and something else: I'm pregnant. Right after the new year, my husband and I will have our second child."

I was right about the enthusiasm. Cheers filled the gym and my varsity players rushed me. How did it feel to release word of the pregnancy beyond our little world of family and friends? It felt amazing. If I knew our girls, from this point the news would go viral.

"Coach Roos! Can we name your baby Kanga?" a returning player shouted, and I laughed. "For now," I said. "Kanga it is." The girls raced off to their courts as my coaches came over to congratulate me.

CHAPTER 6

TESTING

———

OUR NEXT DOCTOR'S visit confirmed the routine. I arrived early and found a seat in the waiting room next to one for Jonas. My awkward stage of looking merely overfed was giving way to a pronounced belly, and though it was early, I'd shifted to maternity wear. A woman next to me looked to be in her early thirties too, and I smiled at her

"I'm Tricia," I said.

"Elizabeth."

"When are you due?"

She let a dated *Parenting* magazine slip to her lap. "First of January. You?"

"Jan five," I said. "Maybe we'll see each other here and at the hospital."

This pregnancy ride was too good not to sweep in every other traveler on the train. Two excited moms-to-be began to exchange numbers when Jonas arrived and Janet called my name. We followed our West Texas technician downstairs into the room where I knew to lie on the gurney and pull up my shirt. She rolled her chair to where

I lay. This time from an oversized tube she squeezed a gob of cold lubricant onto my belly and smeared it like Cameron with finger paints. With her other hand she guided a long wand over my belly. And it happened again. The sounds of a little heartbeat filled the room and our child's image showed on the screen. Still wielding the wand, Janet clicked, noted, measured my baby's head, body, legs and available arms . . . but unlike our first visit, a shadow passed her face.

"What do you think?" I said. "Everything okay?"

"Sure, looks good." Her eyes stayed on the screen. "The baby's a little small, but still in the range of normal, so I wouldn't worry right now."

A few more clicks and she offhandedly said, "Want to know what I think the gender is?" Jonas and I hadn't anticipated knowing this early, but I lived with my fingers crossed, and I said yes.

"I'm not always right, but I'm pretty accurate," Janet twanged. "I say it's a girl."

All along, Jonas's only concern had been for a healthy child, and for weeks I'd claimed no preference. But we had Cameron, and I confess I wanted, I *longed* for, a little girl. I heard Janet's prediction, and salt tears wet my cheeks. She looked at me and warned again that she could be wrong, but her words had their effect. A few minutes later, my shirt down and my heart racing, Jonas and I took the steep stairs to meet with Dr. Martin, me holding the newest roll of sonogram images of our little Kanga.

She was a bean still, but a bigger bean with miniature legs and arms. Her body was more defined. We had profile pictures of her face—maybe it was her face—and I could swear I saw chubby cheeks.

Dr. Martin's energy this time spun on a checklist of questions. I was entering my second trimester, sometimes called the honeymoon period of gradual growth from weeks thirteen to twenty-seven. All healthy. All on schedule. We were saying goodbyes when she tossed in, "I have something to show you. Can you hang on a few minutes?"

She left the room and came back with a brochure. "There's a

lot of new technology out there," she said, handing it to me. "A blood test called cfDNA also tells the baby's gender. Since you're both eager to know, would you want to stay a few minutes and do it today?"

Ask me to hit the ground for a do-or-die volleyball shot, and I'm rolling. Ask me to stand between a hurricane and Cameron, and I'm your stone wall. Show me a tiny needle, and I look away and break a sweat. In a flu shot at school, the nurse has to hold my hand. In a blood sample, for goodness' sake, you see the body's fluid surge into the needle's canister . . . but the desire to know our new child's gender had moved to the head of the line.

"Any risks, anything to worry about?" I asked her. It was worth a check.

"Not at all," Dr. Martin said routinely. "In fact, the test verifies a panel of other things like Down Syndrome."

Down Syndrome. Until now I'd thought of nothing but normal, and the words pulled at my sleeve. "Am I at high risk for anything?"

"You're thirty-one years old," Dr. Martin said. "High-risk pregnancies are mostly among women thirty-five and older, or women with other health issues. I knew you wanted to know the gender." The irony of certain casual moments is how deeply they later burn into our psyches. I can still remember Dr. Martin's looking at me. She said, "No pressure."

Both of my hands wrapped around Jonas's hand. But this was a medical office, for goodness' sake. Every month here hundreds of women took this test, and I could too.

"My nurse will get you started, and we'll have the results in about a week," Dr. Martin said. "You look great."

CHAPTER 7

GETTING HOME

THE CALL CAME when I was far from home.

Except for out-of-town volleyball games, my work has almost no travel. So in the once-in-a-blue-moon event of a professional conference, I'm ready to blow town with my staff and have a little fun.

I did say fun. My love for what I do starts in my DNA, shoots into my soul, and sprouts in every part of my life. When people struggle to separate their jobs and their home lives, while I believe the pain is real, I have to take their word for it that the breakup is necessary.

It may help here to explain that coaching is a fraction of my week. Most of my workdays I'm director of admissions, screening 600 applicants every year for Bishop Lynch High School's 250 freshmen slots. Months of event planning and coordination go into getting fourteen-year-olds through admissions, but my staff is strong and my boss gives me rein to succeed. Now Bishop Lynch was sending six of us to Portland to an AISAP conference—the Association of Independent School Admission Professionals—to take in processes and financial and marketing best practices.

Before Jonas leaves town for a work trip, he's setting out items he anticipates wanting to take. Day-of he's all but ready and cooling his heels, and that's one way to do it. The Saturday of the Bishop Lynch admissions staff takeoff for Portland, I was up early to extract my suitcase from a back closet. The eighty pounds that lingered on my body from Cameron's birth had taken more than a year to lose, leading me to conclude that eating for two is a beautiful lie, and that pregnancy weight-loss management starts during the weight gain. I made sure to pack workout clothes and headphones. At nine o'clock that morning I kissed Jonas and Cameron goodbye. Because this story predates Uber in Dallas, I took a taxi to meet my coworkers at DFW Airport.

Cut now to our plane landing in Portland, and then to us driving out of Portland International Airport to a city of startling contrasts: waterfront vistas and grand hotels bounded by sidewalks of homeless people, most of them seeming to be in their twenties or younger. Walking from our bus to the Benson Hotel, dazzled and dodging vagrants, I happened to make eye contact with a girl on a curb, maybe nineteen years old. Her clothes were torn, her dirty blonde hair was shoved under a blue beanie, her gaze held almost no life. *Where could her parents be,* I thought, and my hand moved to my belly.

Sunday morning, sunny and brisk, I woke early and dressed to run along the river a few blocks from the hotel. In leggings and a striped tank top, looking every bit the part, I grabbed my phone and headphones. Outside, I made my way through sleeping figures and the pungent odor of urine.

Reaching the river, I took an open path for a half mile to a crowd of people in a closed-off scene that looked for all the world like a starting line. In the mid distance a clock flanked by balloons showed six minutes to a community race. Around me, hundreds of runners stretched and milled. Some were pulling off overshirts to hand to their streetside supporters, and I pondered my options. I could go back to the congested downtown sidewalks, or I could crash a run with a mapped route and free water stations. As any rational female out-of-towner running alone would do, I melded into a cluster of paid participants and attempted to look purposeful. My Pandora station was set to running music, the gun sounded, and I vowed to donate later to the charity.

Eagle-eyed spectators on the route may have noticed that my chest was missing a race number, but surely, I reasoned, the fitted tee over my round belly identified me as harmless. Down the Columbia River, past ships and warehouses, through Portland's famed narrow city streets, I ran with the crowd, every mile marker a vision of smiling volunteers holding out cups of cool water. First trimester nausea had kept me out of commission for too long. In the mental rush of this run in a strange city, I crossed the finish line in good time, ate a banana, and posed laughing in a photo with new friends. In the coming months I would study that group shot many times, wondering whether I'd ever smile again.

CHAPTER 8

OCEANS

———————

MONDAY MORNING IN Portland I was up early again for a day of speakers and breakout sessions. In the opulent Benson Hotel lobby of Italian marble, Russian wood, and Austrian chandeliers, six Texans from Bishop Lynch rendezvoused to board the shuttle together for the Catlin Gabel School.

Admissions personnel tend to be both Type A and extroverted. Judging by volume and enthusiasm, our bus ride that day could have been teenagers headed to cheerleading camp. The happy chatter rode up a long crescendo, spinning off energy like sparklers, until we pulled into the resort . . . when all talking died.

Did I say resort? Honest mistake. This conference was at a school of buildings made of contemporary wood-and-glass, spread and nestled into lush landscaping. After two morning sessions, lunch was in a dining hall of vaulted ceilings and log beams. I grabbed my sandwich, chips and drink and joined a cluster of private school administrators from across the US. We were ten minutes into food and notes when my ringing phone said "Dr. Martin's office."

This was it then, the blood test results. I stood up at the table, gestured to my stomach and enunciated, "Gender reveal!" A round of smiles. A round of thumbs up. With a finger in one ear and my phone against the other, I moved to an empty corner of the cafeteria and heard Dr. Martin's voice. How great was that? My doctor was calling me personally.

"Dr. Martin," I fairly shouted. "I didn't expect this call so soon!"

"Hey, Tricia," she said with none of her usual liveliness. Hearing the roar behind me, she said, "Can you find somewhere quiet for us to talk?"

I moved out of the dining hall and down a set of stairs. "Ok, I'm good. Sorry for the noise," I said. My shoulder pressed against a door to exit the building. "I'm in Portland."

"Portland? Portland, Oregon?"

"Yes! With my staff at a work conference. And Dr. Martin, you're making me nervous. Is everything all right?"

That slight pause. "I want to get to the point, Tricia. In the blood test, your baby tests positive for a condition called Trisomy 18. There's a possibility of a false positive, but those are rare."

> "Trisomy 18 is a fatal condition, Tricia. You need to come home as quickly as possible."

Now the scene begins to blur. My doctor was telling me my baby was a girl, but I cut her off. "We can fix that, right?" I said about the condition, my pulse rising. "What does trisomy mean?"

The calm in her voice didn't match her words: "Trisomy 18 is a fatal condition, Tricia. You need to come home as quickly as possible." I'd crossed a campus street to lean against a tree, and now my knees gave way. I couldn't seem to get a full breath.

"Tricia. I'm sorry, but you need to be here to see a specialist. Can you call Jonas and get back to Dallas?"

I must have said okay, and one of us hung up. I fumbled to tap the screen for Jonas, and I heard a ring on his end. An eon later I heard a second ring. I heard Jonas pick up, and I began to sob.

"What's wrong? What's wrong?" he asked in a panic. "Tricia, calm down and tell me what's wrong."

"The baby," I managed to say. "She's not okay." Sounds coming from me were unrecognizable. "I need to come home."

"Go to the airport," he said, his voice tender and urgent. "I'll book your flight. Go straight to the airport. I'll figure it out. I love you. This will be all right."

The first person to find me was Josh. Lunch was over, and in my previous life, he and I would have crossed the green lawns to the next session. That life was over. I tried to stand and didn't make it. I tried to talk and no words came. A local man at the conference drove me to the airport. Someone would see to my things at the hotel.

How Jonas managed, I don't know, but the airline counter had my ticket home. With a layover in Albuquerque, by eleven o'clock, I'd be on a Dallas road in a car with my husband. Until then, waiting in the Portland airport, I did the worst thing: I googled. Again and again. Every article, every report, every story about Trisomy 18, the genetic disorder I'd never heard of, now shredding my life. I'd wipe my sleeve over my eyes and keep reading.

———

Trisomy 18, sometimes called Edward's Syndrome, is an extra chromosome in every cell in a baby's body, slowing development, altering as it goes. For reference, Trisomy 21 is Down Syndrome. Trisomy 18 is rarer and, like Down Syndrome, impossible to prevent or treat. On my phone screen the words "incompatible with life" appeared again and again, and each time I wept.

Harsh storms in Albuquerque were rocking every traveler's schedule. Every flash of lightning brought another half-hour delay, and the sky was a light show. A doctor named Rhonda Walton was the mother of a close friend of mine, and I craved to talk to a non-Google expert. Curled into a hard chair facing the tarmac, I looked down from the storm to key in her number, and she answered—I was grateful for that—but she knew nothing Google hadn't told me. Babies with Trisomy 18 have a welter of heart defects and issues. Most die in the second or third trimester. A live birth was the exception, and my heart was broken.

At the end of forever I boarded a plane for Dallas, taking the first-row aisle seat to bolt as soon as the plane door reopened. My eyes stayed red and swollen. Passengers walking past me looked away, and I marveled to have any tears left. From Dr. Martin's call to my arrival in Dallas, the world was turned inside out. At one o'clock in the morning I climbed into our car and into Jonas's arms, and we wept together. There was little to say now. From New Mexico, as pieces of Dr. Martin's call had come back to me, I'd texted Jonas everything. Texting seemed less final than speaking or hearing the words aloud.

The song on the car radio was *Oceans*, by Hillsong. I knew the lyrics and loved them, and I needed the promise in them. In the dark, Jonas drove and the words and the music washed over me, even as I wondered how my faith would survive.

> *Spirit lead me where my trust is without borders*
> *Let me walk upon the waters*
> *Wherever You would call me*
> *Take me deeper than my feet could ever wander*
> *And my faith will be made stronger*
> *In the presence of my Savior*

Sometime that night I slept. In the morning I woke for an early meeting with the specialist Dr. Martin had referred to—a maternal fetal medicine expert to confirm or deny the genetic blood test results. Some tests turn out to be flawed. However slim, if there was a chance for a false negative, I prayed this agony would be for nothing.

CHAPTER 9

DEEPER

―――――――――

S O MUCH ABOUT pregnancy is waiting.
In a small entry room in a large medical tower, Jonas and I sat
with two other anxious couples in a group I didn't want to belong
to. Jonas filled out the doctor's paperwork while I stared ahead.
Eventually a nurse led us into a room with an oversized recliner and
motioned for me to take it. Jonas moved a stool from near the wall
to my side. In silence he and I waited for the doctor, who came in
offering his sympathy.

I knew this specialist by reputation, this doctor for women
whose pregnancies were in trouble. No one wanted to have to see
him, but they remembered him for his kindness, and that much
I expected. His nurse was a small woman with gentle eyes. In the
corner of the room, she opened a kit of clean packets.

"Let's get to it," the specialist said. Stepping to the corner, he
lowered the room's lights to the glow of the sonogram machine. In
a three-dimensional image, miles ahead of Dr. Martin's technology,
clear as day, we saw our daughter floating in her safe haven.

After more computer clicks, so impersonal in the dark, the

specialist strode to the large screen. "Yep, definitely Trisomy 18," he said. "All the normal markers and indicators." He seemed pleased with his rapid diagnosis, and it seemed to me the end of our world was a good day at work for him. I felt the nurse take my hand. "What do you mean?" I said. "How can you know so quickly?" Jonas and I could barely discern a head or foot. The specialist pointed to swelling in our baby's brain and at the back of her neck, to clenched hands, and to a potentially clubbed foot. Walking back to me, he asked to take a prenatal chorionic villus sampling (CVS) to send to the lab, and I agreed.

With a local anesthetic, he numbed the area around my belly button. Then he produced the world's largest needle and slowly inserted it into my belly. Tears coated my cheeks, and I closed my eyes and prayed. The local prevented my feeling the needle entering my body, but as it pierced the placenta, I winced at the pain and cramping.

"Another minute," he said. "Almost done."

When they had their sample, the nurse left while I brushed off tears of frustration. I felt violated, discounted, but determined on my child's behalf.

"What now, doctor?" Jonas asked.

Sitting on the stool, the specialist pushed back from where I still lay reclined. "Do you have other children?" he said.

Jonas told him we had a three-and-a-half-year-old son named Cameron.

"You want a sibling for Cameron?"

Jonas and I looked at each other, confused. "Of course," I said. "We've wanted another baby so he could have a sibling."

"Then I recommend you get this pregnancy over fast and move on to give your son a new brother or sister."

Unsteadied by the past half hour, Jonas and I felt the words like a knockout blow. Get it over? Move forward? Was he advising us to abort our child to speed up Cameron's having a healthy sibling? If I was hearing right, in the estimation of one of the city's top physicians, our child was a plastic bag in a bush in a vacant lot, a misuse of time and resources. I left the medical office more broken and dazed than at any time in my life.

In the car on the drive home *Oceans* played again.

CHAPTER 10

EMAIL

———————————

FOR A WEEK I cried more than I knew a person could cry, the worry working on me like a stimulant, keeping me agitated and awake. I worried whether my daughter had a heartbeat. I worried about what was happening in her body and mine. I worried over every decision we faced.

For days Jonas and I declined visitors to try to think. Should we end the pregnancy? Was my health at stake? If our daughter survived, would her care break our finances? Every question unleashed more twists in a story with no good ending. But even as I say that, even as the world seemed to crumble around us, something else was at work.

As a child, I had been dreadfully shy. In grade school, my parents tell me, I said almost nothing and showed no interest in sports. My kindergarten teacher couldn't file progress reports on me because I wouldn't talk to her. But then in middle school I became outgoing and competitive. By high school I was into every sport in every season: cross country, volleyball, basketball, track, tennis, cheerleading.

And sports taught me to persevere. To mourn the loss of a game or a match the next day in practice was to waste a day of practice. The thing was to get back to work. Other athletes might be taller and faster than me, but no one practiced or played harder or with better attitude. By sheer will, I did more than I or anyone else thought I could, and those mental muscles would serve me now. If I couldn't see the finish line or know the score or even all the rules of the game, I'd press on because that's what you do. This was our daughter. Quitting on her made no sense.

And slowly, imperceptibly, the darkness in our days began to lift, and worry segued into hunger for information. I resolved to know everything possible about Trisomy 18. Whatever came, I would push back. I would find the good.

My theory about accepting a challenge is that after you commit to it, signposts spring up that don't show the sidelines. Besides reading, I sought out Trisomy 18 parents and doctors and medical professionals. After Jonas and I confided in a few people, the wife of one of his co-workers linked us to a woman named Allison, the mother of a Trisomy 18 daughter named Quinn, who had lived for six months. My first call to Allison lasted for hours—mostly me talking and her crying with me. When she described her pregnancy to me, and her time with Quinn, I wept.

"Was it worth it?" I asked her. "If you'd had the chance, would you have done anything different?" From the daylight end of a long dark tunnel, she told me every second was worth it, and yes, she'd do it all again. She talked about trusting God's plans over her own— easier said than done—and I fiercely valued what she could tell me.

We were still in week one. The AISAP conference in Portland was still going on, enabling me to suffer the worst days without losing ground at work. In a few days, at the end of tears, prayers, and long talks, Jonas and I agreed we would not try to hide our news. Volleyball camp started the next Monday, and for my own clarity,

I began to draft an email to my coworkers. To try to tell people individually and in person would have been impossible. On Friday, July 18, I emailed one letter to a long list of friends and coworkers.

Good Morning,

On Monday, July 14, at noon, if you'd asked me, I would have said my life was nearly perfect. I love my husband, our church, my wild little three-year-old, and my job. I was thrilled to be pregnant (3.5 months), and I hoped for a girl.

By 12:45 p.m. that day, everything had changed. While I was in Portland at a work conference, my doctor's office called to tell me that I am carrying a girl who has Trisomy 18, a lethal disease with a 90% chance of death during pregnancy. If I should deliver full term, she'd likely pass away within minutes or hours of the birth. In rare cases babies live a little longer, but only a little, and there is no cure.

Since Tuesday, every medical professional has recommended that Jonas and I end the pregnancy. Trisomy 18 is the one chromosome disease even the Baylor ethics board will approve to terminate. Unless it seriously threatens my health, however, that won't happen. God makes no accidents, and our daughter's return to heaven will be on his timing, not ours.

So, you'll see me at BL in my office, in the gym, around the school, looking pregnant for up to the next 5 1/2 months. If at any point in that time she passes, I will go through normal labor and delivery. In the rare case that I make it full term and get to meet her, it will probably be only a few precious moments. In the extreme case that she lives a few weeks or months, she will require 24-hour care, and though that scares me, I'll do whatever God asks.

We appreciate your prayers and support. We want no special treatment, but rumors spread, and I'd rather you hear this from me. We will be faithful to God and praise him for all our blessings. We're prepared for the path he's laid before us.

In closing, from my best friend, Laura, below is the reading in *Jesus Calling* for July 14—the day I got the news—which I consider to be no coincidence. It has made me

strong through the last few days,
and it continues to inspire me.

July 14

*Keep walking with Me along the path
I have chosen for you. Your desire
to live close to Me is a delight to
My heart. I could instantly grant
you the spiritual riches you desire,
but that is not My way for you.
Together we will forge a pathway
up the high mountain. The journey
is arduous at times, and you are
weak. Someday you will dance light
footed on the high peaks; but for
now, your walk is often plodding
and heavy. All I require of you is
to take the next step, clinging to
My hand for strength and direction.
Though the path is difficult and
the scenery dull at the moment,
there are sparkling surprises just
around the bend. Stay on the path I
have selected for you. It is truly
the path of Life. Psalm 37:23-24;
Psalm 16:11*

Sincerely,
Tricia Roos

Less than a week after Dr. Martin's call, I was back at work,
hungry for routine and activity and no more days in bed—and
activity I got. The gym and my office are maybe a hundred

yards apart. For four consecutive twelve-hour days, I sped—no, ricocheted—between my admissions responsibilities and three volleyball camps. Call it mania; call it a godsend. As volleyball camp began, I could see the girls had read my email, or at least their parents had. The high spirits of my June announcement at the volleyball clinic were gone. Unless I addressed our latest turn of events head on, the awkwardness would only grow.

The first morning of camp I gathered the girls in a huddle. "Ladies," I said, "I assume you know about my pregnancy and my daughter." Heads bobbed. Several of the girls looked at the ground, unsure, perhaps, how to meet my eyes.

"I'm sad," I said, "but I'm also hopeful that God has a bigger purpose for my daughter's life and for mine. The only thing I ask is that you make volleyball a place for me to forget about everything else. Even when you or I have bad days, we can come here with good attitudes."

Another group nod, and a perceptible change in mood. The girls had a way to help me now. Anxiety and awkwardness could drop back. That week the teamwork and fun outdid anything in my career. Practice *was* an escape, and our time together grew sacred. Maybe it was coincidence, maybe it was love, but here was my therapy—mine and theirs. What high school sports had given me I could pass on to these girls. Whatever happened, this season already was a gift.

CHAPTER 11

GRACE

———

AS ITS MASTHEAD says, The Texas Catholic is the newspaper of record for the Diocese of Dallas, home to 1.2 million-plus Catholics in eighty parishes that stir into a community I love. Bishop Lynch High School, where I'd worked for more than a decade, opened in 1963, founded as a college-prep school. Bishop Joseph Lynch was a massively influential figure in Dallas. His legacy extends across hundreds of schools and churches. This particular school started with 350 students and today, grades nine through twelve, has more than a thousand.

A Christian academy obviously aims past just getting its graduates into good colleges. Our students learn not just what to do but who to be, things pivotal to my being there. In my first week back since Dr. Martin's call, The Texas Catholic showed up in a stack of publications in our office. I thought about their reports from our school, always about where faith meets life, even in the sports coverage. Given my research into Trisomy 18, and the doctors who had urged me to terminate the pregnancy, a thought came to me about the journey Jonas and I were on.

and meeting Jonas, Cameron's arrival, and now my pregnancy. I told about Cameron's asking me for a lady baby, and then I dropped my guard. Since Dr. Martin's call until this moment, I had sent an email, held a camp, held volleyball scrimmages, and showed up for work, always from an emotional distance.

"I'll be honest," I said now. "The diagnosis is hard, and I'm broken by it. If I have days when I can't manage or I seem distracted, I worry I'll hurt your season. I want to be there for you, but I may fall short. I hope you can understand and forgive me."

Tears stung my eyes. Two of my captains volunteered that no matter what, they would support me and give everything on the court. As a team we rose to our feet and moved into a hug, a moment of love and respect against a Texas landscape.

This is what we'd come for. Every load ahead would lighten with the support of these players and assistant coaches. My fear of losing focus in practices and games was real, but now the team allowed for it. For the first time since "the call," I could smile and even laugh. That afternoon we played volleyball, swam in the lake, judged stunts off the diving board at the pool, and basked in who we were together. Late that night the girls fell into bed and slept hard.

On Sunday I woke early to read scripture. After some time alone, I roused the team for a service held by a Methodist men's retreat. Uncomplaining and quiet, the girls tumbled out of their bunks and followed a narrow path to a spot near the shore. From the water a cool breeze whispered in and a cross towered over the blue lake. The Methodist men read scriptures and we all sang hymns, one a haunting acapella rendition of *Amazing Grace*. In the hope and the surrender of the moment, I sensed the presence of the Holy Spirit, and I let myself hope.

CHAPTER 12

WATER

———

VOLLEYBALL SEASON LEAPT to life with two matches a week and tourneys in August. Our girls soared on the courts, doubled down in practice, and in the rhythm of our schedule, the hard parts of my life moved to the margins. But that was at school. At home, in the car, at the grocery store or nail salon, the pressure in my chest sometimes grew so intense I wanted to give up.

Most Trisomy 18 babies die in utero, but this far into pregnancy my body would give birth, and that terrified me. When I prayed, what should I ask for? For the miracle of a healthy baby? For my daughter to make it full term? For her to live some span of time? Eventually the only prayer that made sense was for God's will. No desperate pleas for length of life, just *thy will be done*. Most nights I fell to sleep in tears, asking for my child to survive the night and live one more day.

Some days it helped to go out for a run, but in the unforgiving heat of a Texas summer, my swollen belly was closing off that outlet. One Sunday afternoon near the end of August, when an unseen hand dials the temperature to full blast, I was particularly blue.

Against Jonas's wishes, I put on my running shoes and left the house. The day was in the mid-nineties, sun-flooded and humid. My departing words, I think, were that I'd stay in the neighborhood and be back soon.

Typically, on a run I listen to Christian music and pray, but today I jogged and seethed. *Why?* I shouted in my head. *Why give us an innocent baby and let her die? Where are you? Haven't I tried to do the right things?*

Tears, so much a part of my days now, coursed down my face. My feet picked up the pace. At some point, too many miles from home, parched, and with no water in sight, I came to a stop, looked around, and panicked. I kicked myself for losing track of the distance, and I racked my brain. I knew this route. The only way back was the way I'd come. The closest water fountain was another mile, maybe two, toward White Rock Lake. I didn't want Jonas to know I'd come this far, and I didn't want him to have to come pick me up.

What to do? What? What? What? A thought came to me that a Bishop Lynch grad, a former volleyball player, lived nearby and that her number was in my phone. I'd ask her if I could come to her house, grab a glass of water to cool down, and then head home. I scrolled through my contacts and tapped, and a familiar voice answered.

"Nicole!" I said, all but reaching through the phone. "Nicole, hey, it's Coach Roos. This is really random, but I'm on a run and a few blocks from you. I wonder if I could just stop by for a glass of water. It's so hot, and I forgot to bring a bottle." At least two years had passed since I'd seen her. Who knew what she was thinking?

"I'm so sorry!" she was saying, and I could hear her voice rise to a *no*. "I'm not home right now, Coach Roos! I'm at my aunt's house babysitting."

Everything inside me sank. "No problem," I said, trying to mask my desperation. I needed more to say but nothing would come.

"If you want, you could come to my aunt's house," I heard her say now. "It's pretty close to mine."

A thin slice of hope. "Well, if that's not weird," I said. "I'm so hot and thirsty, and that would be awesome."

"Where are you so I can give you directions?"

Standing at an intersection, I squinted at the street signs in front of me. I said, "I'm at the corner of Fischer and Dalgreen."

"Are you kidding me?"

"Yeah, that's where I am right now."

"Turn to your right," Nicole said. "You're in front of my aunt's house. I'll open the gate and come out."

And there we both were. As I'd run and shaken my fist at God, as I lost myself in lashing out, he was leading me to water, and his message staggered me: "I've got you. I will provide for you. You will be okay."

Later I thought of Jesus' calling himself the Bread of Life. He said whoever comes to him will never go hungry, whoever believes in him will never thirst.

A tall gate swung open to a Mediterranean-style mansion, and a former student of mine stepped out holding an oversized tumbler of fresh water in crushed ice. Both of us knew something extraordinary had just happened. I ran home with no complaining, no whining about my situation and, it's worth mentioning, no fatigue.

CHAPTER 13

VISION

———

WHAT'S IN A name? I'll tell you. Identity. Belonging. Maybe a whole life story. I knew our daughter's name had to serve extra duty, and for weeks Jonas and I put off choosing it. I'd long loved "Andie," but that wasn't this girl's name. For hours in the evenings I googled list after list of names, until the day I came to Annabelle, meaning grace and beauty, and a key piece snapped into place. Too many experts would dismiss our daughter's life for her differences, but she was gracefully beautiful. She was our Annabelle, and now we knew her by name.

The Texas Catholic's ongoing coverage had drawn the interest of WFAA-TV, the local ABC News affiliate, and The Dallas Morning News, and the timing was good. Emotionally, Jonas and I were better able now to talk publicly about how our decision played out in our daily lives. The WFAA story aired on September 12. The Morning News ran a frontpage piece on September 23, two days before my birthday. I was in my office that morning, turning on my computer, when Josh burst in.

"You see the Morning News?"

"Not yet. Just logging on."

"Whatever you do," Josh said, "don't read the comments."

I looked up to see if he was joking. Like the day Dr. Martin called me with Annabelle's diagnosis, when I googled Trisomy 18 until every new article or website could only repeat what I already knew, information was my default.

"Josh," I said, "you do realize that now I *have* to read these comments?"

He pulled a chair to my desk. "I'm staying with you, then," he said.

I keyed in "Dallas News," and a front page filled the screen. I saw a picture of me tossing a volleyball midair, which I liked. The headline said, "Bishop Lynch coach's courage despite unborn baby's defect inspires team." The article was written well. The journalist *got* us and, most important, got the facts. What had Josh so worked up?

Then I reached the end of the piece and hundreds of comments. Many were positive. Many more were not just negative but shooting to kill. One person would rail against our decision and dozens more would weigh in, forming a long tail of anger. Strangers called me cruel, arrogant, selfish for carrying a child I knew would die. People said I was keeping an innocent child in pain.

"I told you," Josh said, and I pushed my chair back from the screen.

"People can have their opinions," I said, "but wow." Until now, not once had I considered that our story might unleash pure meanness—just as I was beginning to feel hopeful again.

"We're done," Jonas said when I called him. Too much life in a fishbowl, too much attention in a fell swoop. It was one thing to normalize pain and tough decisions. It was one thing to talk about sacrifice, to make it okay for others to broach exceptional pregnancies. We would not set ourselves up for shooting practice.

Jonas is private and protective, as I've said, but I hadn't given up, and the pull between us now had us back at square one. By nature

I'm a coach, a connector, a communicator. What life teaches me I teach others. Our story had more chapters . . . but I was hurt, too.

As the barbs from the newspaper comments continued to dig in, it helped me to go to my office and keep my head down. Two or three days after the article ran, I was planning a volleyball practice around an upcoming admissions event when my desk phone rang. The caller ID said RICK SANTORUM. I knew the name somehow, an applicant's parent, maybe. Wait, no, the guy who ran for president. But not that guy, surely. Probably someone with the same name, or some political recording.

"Admissions office," I said, "This is Tricia."

"Tricia, this is Karen Santorum. I saw the story in the paper about your daughter with Trisomy 18." As the voice spoke, I googled. This Karen Santorum was married to the presidential candidate. She said more, and my eyes scanned more. The Santorums' daughter, Bella, has Trisomy 18. Karen stayed with the pregnancy, and now Bella was six years old.

What a kindness for her to call. And what was going on? Karen Santorum was inviting me to stay in touch. She promised to mail an advance copy of *Bella's Gift*, the book she'd just written. We hung up, and I stared. Another call when I needed it. A child with Trisomy 18 alive and loved. Whether or not that could be Annabelle's story, it was enough to know that Bella was a blessing.

And this seemed to be the pattern. When I shook my fist at God, he took me by the hand. When I thought I was taking a hit, I was being led. At first brush, the news coverage made us want to lock our doors and toss our phones in the nearest creek. But God turns hurt on its head. Now the things that hurt us led us to a foxhole community of goodness, people ahead of us on our journey. That week I also learned about a Facebook group dedicated to parents with trisomy children, introducing me to unsung warriors like two ladies in the area who held an annual run

> But God turns hurt on its head.

to raise money and awareness. This fierce fellowship was dedicated to praying, listening and helping in any way possible.

At home Jonas and I focused on Cameron's understanding that his prayers for a lady baby had been answered but that Annabelle might also return to heaven. Jesus used a child to illustrate the way all of us are to trust God, and Cameron was our ever-present visual aid. His lady baby came from heaven, where God is. If God brought her back early, we'd miss her, but she'd be with him. Cameron listened to us, and he talked about his sister in ways uncanny for a soul of only three and a half years. Every day he spoke to Annabelle in my stomach, telling her he loved her and prayed for her.

———

Besides our monthly checkups with Dr. Martin, she sent us to a special center for 3-D sonograms to track Annabelle's progress. Updates had their purpose, but I was going because the video clarity would be the closest I might ever get to personal visits with Annabelle.

What I expected from the rest of the experience, I can't say. It wasn't what Jonas and I walked into: a waiting room of women, mostly alone, mostly looking as if their lives were hard in the extreme. We found seats next to an untouched stack of National Geographics, and we waited until a nurse with purple and blonde hair opened a door and called our names. From there we walked a long, dim hallway to a wide room of screens and equipment.

Screens and equipment and nothing more. No pictures on walls, no signs of attempts at comfort. And no matter, I reasoned. At twenty weeks, midway through my pregnancy, Annabelle was the size of a sweet potato and highly visible on screen. In a few minutes, we were joined by a doctor who displayed no humor, no kindness, no words. My job was to lay on the table while she squirted the gel and worked the wand across my belly. In the cavernous room, the only sounds were her gasps and moans.

"Wow, not good." [Pause.] "Okay, this looks bad."

I waited for our expert to also address the owner of the belly when Jonas said, "Doctor, would you share some of your findings so we can understand what we're seeing?"

She looked up then with a face that seemed to say we were asking for the obvious. With the cursor on the screen, she circled a shape over and over. "Look at this," she said. "This is the baby's heart. Two chambers, not four. You don't get to full term with this."

The nurse with the purple hair spoke up. "We can induce you any time. It's okay to do that if you want."

I hoisted to my elbows for eye contact first with the doctor and then with her assistant. I said, "We are not terminating my pregnancy. If we induce now, there is zero chance of survival. We will not do that."

Our doctor half shrugged. "Look at her brain," she said. "White spots everywhere. See?"

"I see the white spots," I said testily. I knew they could indicate an absence of brain matter.

"It's extremely rare for those to go away now. The body can't function if the brain isn't telling it what to do," the doctor said.

No more. No more sharing our limited time with Annabelle with a nurse telling me to induce early and a doctor reminding me, with no signs of charity, that our situation was grim.

Yes, I get it. Her development is abnormal. She's small. Her heart has two chambers instead of four. Her brain has spots. She is ours. I want to love her as long as I can, and to see her and know her, if only in these sonograms.

A half hour later, as Jonas pulled out of the clinic parking lot, I called Dr. Martin. She listened to me describe the visit, then asked whether I'd seen the female or male physician. Female, I said. Go again, Dr. Martin urged, and ask for Dr. Magee, the male doctor. And for her sake, I agreed.

Everything happens for a reason, but reasons can stay elusive. One bitter night of intense mental pain I cried myself to sleep, as I often did. The next morning, I woke from a dream so intense I knew I had to write it down.

As I was growing up, my favorite pet was a white cockapoo named Tara—my comfort in my parent's divorce, the constant in our many moves, a close friend in my rocky teenage years. When I was sick or blue, regardless of any activity around us, Tara stayed at my side. During my freshman year in college when she was put down, I drove home to be at her side. I wrote a love letter to her and buried it with her.

In my dream, Tara led me to a beautiful field and talked to me, all of it making perfect sense. She told me something would happen sooner than Jonas and I expected, and I assumed she meant Annabelle's birth. In the dream that didn't scare or sadden me.

She told me not to let fear of medical costs affect our care for Annabelle, a point of contention for Jonas and me because both of us felt overwhelmed. The finances would work out, Tara said. She advised me to delay a planned addition to our house, at the time just shy of 1,500 square feet. When we'd learned I was pregnant, Jonas and I had paid an architect to help us build on, and we were still wrangling the details. Let it go, she told me. We'd need our energy for the days coming. She said Annabelle had no pain and that her life would have great value.

Then we were in the sanctuary in my church, where Tara led me to the front. We were at a funeral, a packed house of my family and friends, all praising and worshiping and rejoicing. Around us a tremendous light shone through the stained glass.

"Annabelle will bring people to Jesus, Tricia," Tara said. "You've been abundantly blessed." *Abundantly blessed.* She said it several times, and it repeated in my head.

The last thing she said was to hold to my faith. Through the pain now and the pain to come, she said, "Trust the Lord. You will be abundantly blessed." As the dream faded, my childhood friend told me she missed me and watched over me. That morning as I woke up, despite the difficulties of the past months, I knew my pregnancy was a blessing. I would cling to God. If he could give me a dream to tell me Annabelle's life had purpose, I would trust him with her days.

CHAPTER 14

UNDEFEATED

———

B Y EARLY OCTOBER temperatures in Dallas were, well, less hot, and Bishop Lynch girls volleyball was breaking records—every match another case of a team willing itself to win state.

Leading into the playoffs, in our district of nine schools, every team plays each other twice. Our record was 14-0 with two district matches left when we had our final home game of the season, also senior night to honor the young ladies and parents in our program for the past four years. We faced off with Bishop Dunne High School, a beloved cross-town rival whose coach was in his own off-court struggle with his wife's health concerns.

The Bishop Dunne players filed from their locker room to the center court pausing every few yards to gaze up and around at our new facilities. For more than fifty years, every sport at our school had operated out of one gym so small, so classically old, that production crews filmed commercials in it. Now after a year of construction, our games rocked and roared in not just a gym but a massive competition center able to seat up to 1,500 fans. Ninety banners dropped from its cavernous ceiling to broadcast ninety state championships. Every district team coming in for the first time had the same slack-jawed response. Watching it never got old.

After tonight, all remaining games would be on neutral courts, so this also was our film crew's last home event. Sometime during the team warmup an "on the way" text came from The Texas Catholic crew, and I smiled. Since that first weekend at the lake, I'd grown used to my entourage, and I loved them.

I slid my phone into my pocket, saying half aloud, *this is it.* A few matches to go, and then no volleyball to block out the rest of my life. For three months I'd drafted on our undefeated district season, on postgame interviews and wins, on smiles and high fives. But sports coverage was about to give way to my unborn daughter's story, and . . .

And for now, I'd concentrate on the match.

Volleyball may be the only national sport still messing with the rules. In 2003, high school girls volleyball instituted rally scoring to grant a point at every volley, which fans love. Girls in general love volleyball, I think, because the contact is mostly group hugs between points. Opponents stay on the other side of the net, not in your face when you're trying to shoot or blocking your path as you try to move downcourt. Volleyball practices skip the long laps in other sports for quick sprints. The drills are to sharpen technique—serving, passing, setting, hitting—and rapid response. In high school volleyball, the winner in a match is the side that takes three of five sets and scores at least twenty-five points a set (that much was settled in 2008), ahead by at least two points.

On the October night of our final home game of 2014, the lead bandied between Bishop Lynch and Bishop Dunne until my girls took the first set and found their stride. More high fives, more smiles, more seamless domination. In the third set, I rotated in every player with extra time for graduating seniors. The gym was new but the girls were veterans and nostalgia ran high. Josh spoke into the mic on my collar: "Even with those pesky Texas Catholic people, we had a great season," he said. Across the gym, Seth rolled his eyes and laughed.

And into the playoffs went Bishop Lynch volleyball team with a 16-0 district record, earning top seed for rounds one and two in Salado, forty-five minutes south of Waco. Rounds three and four, the semi-finals and finals, would be in Corsicana, an hour outside of Dallas. The time away promised fun with the players and full distraction with the games, and I clung to it.

On the Halloween morning of our departure for round one, the girls wore their costumes to school, and I wore mine. I'd bought an orange tee shirt at a craft store, glued black-felt eyes and a mouth on the lower half of it, and outfitted my belly as a pumpkin topped with a pink sequined bow.

"Lookin' good, Annabelle," I said, patting the nose.

———

My tradition for playoffs is to have a guest speaker—typically a fellow coach or leader at Bishop Lynch—send us out the door. This year, with a streak on the line, the speaker had to *get* the pressures my players were under and the pressure I lived with, and we had the guy. On Halloween afternoon, before loading onto the bus, as the girls took seats on locker room benches, I introduced our head women's basketball coach, Andy Zihlman, Bishop Lynch's institution within an institution.

Coach Zihlman was a homegrown grad who'd returned in 1978 to head the women's program, so far earning twenty-six state titles to my three. I was a raw twenty-four-year-old when he entrusted me with the volleyball program, a year after my work in his basketball program gave me a front row seat to how teams and seasons can end at the top of their game. I told the girls that a man whose teams exemplified grace under pressure would speak to them, and Coach Z stood up in his iconic black polo shirt and khakis.

He peered over his glasses and then took them off. "We at the school and those in the athletic department are proud of what you've accomplished so far," he said. "It's not only a testament to yourselves, Coach Roos, and the volleyball program, but to Bishop Lynch High School and how you carry yourselves on the court and off."

All true. The girls felt the moment and the words. From my chair at the left of the door, I watched their young faces—excited, scared, intent.

He spoke of character and competition. Near the end his voice broke. A streak is a charge to keep, he said. He knew the exceptional season and the circumstances behind this moment. "I'm proud of y'all for supporting this lady, and for what she's gone through—the testament she is to all of us and to our school," he said. "Good luck and go Friars!"

> Pushing back tears, I smiled and tried to freeze the moment in my mind.

The room erupted, and every player left the locker room holding a red rose from Coach Zihlman. I brought up the rear with a hug for this father figure and a whispered "Thanks Z." Just outside the door, lining the stairs to the exit, hundreds of students cheered, clapped, and passed out high fives. Pushing back tears, I smiled and tried to freeze the moment in my mind.

We were on the road and well beyond Dallas when muffled whispers and arguing floated up from the back of the bus. In a few minutes, a team captain named Morgan came to where I sat in the front seat with Josh.

"Coach Roos, we have a proposition," she said. "If we win this afternoon, can we please, please go to the haunted house tonight?"

In my third trimester, most nights I could barely get to eight o'clock. Getting teenagers to a haunted house in the cold to face down a zombie with a chainsaw seemed especially unlikely, and I turned to Josh.

"What do you think?" I said to my assistant with the heart of a twelve-year-old boy. "You want to take them if we win our match?"

"Oh yeah," he said.

Morgan's head whipped toward the back of the bus. "They said YES!" she cried and got a mixed response. The debate may have been over who wanted to go, but the group had decided. If getting frightened out of their wits helped them clinch the early playoffs, it didn't scare me.

The bus rolled on, and I soaked in the girls' chatter until Salado signs appeared, signaling to us that the end truly was near. Win it and return to Dallas to prepare for state; lose and return empty handed—call the season a wrap. Annabelle was still with us, and that was no small thing. From habit I looked at the biggest part of me and patted it. The bus pulled up at Salado High School, and we clambered into the aisles. The team's two male managers shouted above the noise. "Coach Roos, since it's Halloween and we want the girls to play relaxed, can we wear our costumes to the game?"

Alvin and Justin were top-notch managers, masters at ginning up pregame spirit. They had the girls' respect. I had a history of using male volleyball players as varsity managers in part because Bishop Lynch had no boys volleyball team. The boys got to play a sport they loved, they competed with the girls in practice, and they supported our team in its matches.

"Well, it's your senior year, and you guys have been pretty awesome. So yes, Batman and Robin, go for it!" With a high five the boys disappeared to get into costume and surprise the team, and our memorable weekend continued to churn out highlights.

Inside the school gymnasium, the opposing teams warmed up for round one. Our pregame swings were the best I'd seen. Our energy seemed unmatched. Spread out across from us, the Beaumont Kelly High School team served. After a quick side-out, Francesca Goncalves served twenty-three unanswered points. The Bishop

Lynch team ticked like a gold watch and before we knew it, the score was 24-0.

Rally scoring makes a shutout almost impossible; certainly, I'd never coached one. It's too easy for a player to make a small mistake and open a point. But this game was mistake-free. On set point, Francesca fired a missile to the Beaumont outside hitter, our opponent popped a quick pass, set and hit, and the ball kissed Haley Puddy's fingertips. The other team scored, and even their parents moaned. We laughed, and one point later switched sides, up one set to zero.

Bishop Lynch intended to win, and win we did: 25-1, 25-9, and 25-15, in three straight sets, rotating every girl into play. Batman and Robin lapped the gym while the team huddle sent up an extra cheer, which Josh may have joined, for the ghouls and zombies in their near future. Jonas had brought Cameron, and as my team reviewed evening plans in the huddle, a small towhead weaseled into the center. "Cameron!" a few of the girls shouted, and he beamed.

"Good job, ladies!" he shouted. I grabbed my boy for a hug impossible now with my large stomach and pulled him into a side squeeze. "Love you, buddy!"

"Love you, Annabelle!" he said, wrapping his arms around my stomach.

Two hours later the winning team was in costumes and loaded onto the bus for the Waco haunted house. "Josh, you're in total charge or else," I warned. "Keep them together and in one piece!"

My assistant coach's face was a picture of bliss. "We'll be fine! See you tomorrow!" The bus pulled away, leaving Jonas and me to a supercharged little boy overdue to trick-or-treat. Our plans were to ride the family-Halloween coattails of a former college roommate of mine named Nicole, now living about twenty miles from Salado.

Nicole and I never had to be alike or together to be close. In college her biology major crowded her desk with science books and her days with library and lab time. In the business school, my energies went to group projects and endless papers for my PR minor.

Our bond and our first meeting started at the Baylor club volleyball team, the college version of my favorite sport since high school.

Almost as soon as I arrived at Baylor for my freshman year, I'd headed for the intramural scene where I found a flyer about a new club volleyball program. Put me in, coach. We played and traveled with time left over for life and just enough commitment to build lasting friendships. Nicole and I both loved fun; we both played to win. We gave everything on the court, and in class demanded laughter in the bargain or why do it. Whether I distracted her from studies more or she distracted me would be an entertaining debate, but both of us got out with decent GPAs.

Now she and her husband, Garrett, lived in a quaint neighborhood outside Temple, another exit off I-35 toward Austin. Their little girl, Hannah, was two years old, and their neighborhood was ground zero for kids and yard decorations. Nicole and I hugged and picked up as if our last visit had been the week before, except she was a PA now—a physician's assistant—knowledgeable in my kind of pregnancy. How much did I know about this stage, she asked me. What were the doctors saying about the birth? What were my plans? The keen interest so characteristic of Nicole now ran on medical training.

"Honestly I don't know," I said, and sighed. "I'm so focused on this volleyball season I haven't thought that far. I know I have to, but I'm not ready."

Mostly I was putting off my birth plan, a document that would outline our desires for every potential scenario related to Annabelle's birth, making her death too real to me. I only wanted to think of her in my womb . . . and Nicole tapped the brakes.

"You'll know what to do when the time comes," she said gently. "And I guess there's no better time to tell you we're expecting our second child too."

I hugged and congratulated her, and she gave me a long look. "Seriously," I said. "I'm happy for you, and Hannah gets to be a big sister!"

Trick-or-treating came to a sticky-fingered and messy-faced end. We said goodbye and draped a worn out three-year-old into his car seat. That night someone who knew me well had gotten through my defenses, and candor these days was unusual for me. My close friends, I held tight. Super tight. At a dinner party, a birthday event, or any occasion, I avoided acquaintances or strangers who might judge me for keeping Annabelle or ask me for details. I was a Type A extrovert hiding from social situations, and that scared me too. Was it okay to want to pull into a cave? More to think about after volleyball season.

The next morning my players wandered into breakfast in the hotel lobby in groups of four, by room, wearing PJs and warm blankets, looking relatively rested. "You guys ready to play?" I said to a round of "yeps" and "yeahs" —good enough for teen girls on a Saturday before noon. "Let's finish breakfast, and then change and grab your bags," I said. "We'll check out on our way to the gym to win!"

Slightly louder "yeahs" this time, and I turned to Josh, who was drinking coffee across from me, to ask about the haunted house. It had almost slipped my mind, and now he laughed. "Well, I guess it was a success," he said. "Some girls cried, but mostly everyone had a good time."

"Cried?"

"Yeah, these creepy dudes were roaming the parking lot and one jumped on the bus and scared the girls out of their minds. I made him get off the bus, but it was pretty wild."

I had a life-size picture of my hugely pregnant and waddling self in the parking lot, some clown leaping at me from behind a car. I would have punched him or gone into labor on the spot, or both, confirming my decision to deputize Josh.

"Josh," I said, "that is literally my worst nightmare." He laughed and his eyes went to my stomach. "Not your gig," he said.

A few minutes later the girls on the bus had transformed from sleepy teenagers in pajamas to focused athletes ready for St. Anthony's of San Antonio. In their black uniforms, top to toe, everything said machine, and the match played out that way: near-flawless in the first set, winning 25-4, the next two sets similarly dominated, 25-12, and 25-11. Another three-set sweep punched our ticket to the state semifinals in exactly one week.

CHAPTER 15

LIES

———————

BACK IN DALLAS, Monday morning brought my regular checkup with Dr. Martin, and who should be in the waiting room but Elizabeth, the mom-to-be from my second appointment, when I still believed we were on the same train.

In the entire waiting area, the one open seat was across from her. I slipped into it quietly, my eyes on my lap, but it happened anyway.

"Tricia?"

"Elizabeth."

"How are you?" she said sweetly. "I haven't seen you since we were, what, twelve weeks along?"

"Yep, that was when we last saw each other." I looked around the room for a distraction. No happily pregnant woman wants to hear about a baby who might die at any moment.

"I'm great. Things are great," I lied. "How about you?"

"It's been a rough pregnancy, but the baby is tracking big. He may come sooner than later."

Him. We'd met before we knew the genders. "My son is so fun," I said. "You'll love being a boy mom."

"How about you? Did you want to know your gender?"

"We did. It's a girl."

Her eyebrows flew up. "A girl? Oh, so fun! I bet you're picking out clothes and bedding and all kinds of things!"

I have got to get out of here. "It's been really fun," I said.

My daughter would have no baby showers. In our house, nothing was rearranged or added for her. If she came tomorrow, the only thing new would be her.

I excused myself to go to the bathroom. At the end of what I hoped was a long time, I opened the bathroom door and peered out. Elizabeth was gone, thank God. I heard my name called, double thanks to God. The nurse showed me to the room to wait for Dr. Martin, who might also have some insight into my lying and guilt. In our countless appointments, she often doubled as guidance counselor, the person who knew my pregnancy in some ways better than I did.

This time she entered the room with no small talk, none of her usual bounce. She looked at me and cocked her head.

"How are you doing, Tricia?"

"I don't know. It's been tough. I'm more scared about what's going to happen."

"Only natural." She forced a small cough. "I can't know everything you're going through, Tricia, but your job is to stay healthy for the baby. Your blood pressure is high, and we need to manage that better." In her arms a file bulged with reports.

The blood pressure lecture usually came around volleyball games and work stress. Now a week from the state playoffs, I debated whether to mention to her that my blood pressure might be on schedule to soar again. I settled on saying, "I'm trying hard in our matches to not get too excited or stressed, but . . ."

"But what?"

"But our state championship is this weekend." I smiled to shrug off the blood pressure thing.

"I'm happy for you and your team, but unless you can stay calm in your games it won't be pretty," Dr. Martin said. I searched her face for a reason to feel better, and I said I'd work on it.

"Have you worked on your birth plan?"

Busted again. "I wanted to get through the weekend with volleyball and then focus on that," I said. No part of this appointment was going well.

"Next time we need to discuss some of your wishes about the birth," Dr. Martin said firmly. "I know it's hard, but we're getting close."

My head moved up and down. Yes. It was bad to go into labor with no written record of what we wanted to happen. Having given birth once, I was aware that planning sessions don't start during contractions, but nothing seemed to close the distance between me and a formal plan.

After the season.

CHAPTER 16

STATE

————

THAT WEEK, ALL week long, practices were models of high-energy hard work. By Thursday afternoon after school, we were on the bus headed for a good night's pre-game rest in Corsicana. Our semifinal on Friday was against Antonian Prep from San Antonio, an especially strong first opponent.

Corsicana is its own story: sixty miles from Dallas, population 23,000, and short on motels and hotels. For our institution's governing body—The Texas Association of Private and Parochial Schools (TAPPS)—the single objective appeared to be the cheapest prices going. If that meant wedging twenty-four teams from six divisions into a town with no lodging, well, welcome to sunny Corsicana.

And welcome to the fine print of coaching: the travel and hotel reservations work sure to jade the staunchest sports lover. I say that to explain why, when a volleyball parent tipped me off to a Bishop Lynch family with a lake house in Corsicana, I ignored the tip. I said good to know, but our travel team and I had no desire for the girls or me to have to sleep on floors.

When my thanks but no thanks showed up in her cell phone, the mom texted back a link to the website for guests of the "Great House," a 20,000-square-foot castle of Austin stone, dark wood, and a raised-seam roof on land with a horse stable, pool, hot tub, lighted tennis courts, and a sweeping view of the lake. The guest house alone made my home in East Dallas look like an afterthought. Together, the two residences on this property would accommodate my staff, players and managers with room left for a pro football game—and all this in tiny Corsicana, Texas.

I texted the team mom: ARE YOU KIDDING ME??? and got back: *Call immediately and book it.* Corsicana had its points, and the sun that long weekend would shine on our volleyball team.

As for the drive to our host city that afternoon, without a GPS, a bus driver could sneeze and miss the exit. Our bus turned off the highway in the right place and passed long stretches of farmland to finally reach the Shore Seasons gatehouse. From there, another mile of rolling hills and trees led to the grand main house, which, as it came into view, drew audible gasps.

"Meeting in fifteen, everyone!" I shouted as we stopped. "Get your stuff to your rooms and meet up in the living room of the big house!"

I hauled my backpack and suitcase up a long staircase and down a hallway to a spacious master bedroom with a balcony overlooking the living room. Somebody pinch me. In the living room, a wooden chandelier presided over a floor-to-ceiling stone fireplace and all the seating we could want for our meetings. I dropped my bags next to a king-size bed near a bathroom twice the size of our school locker room.

Our girls walked into the living area the way rival teams came into our school's new competition gym back in Dallas. "I want to set the tone for the weekend," I said as they found seats and quieted. "We're here to do our very best to win a state championship, but more important, to have fun and bond and build memories. We've been blessed with a once-in-a-lifetime experience, so make it count."

The return smiles shot to my heart. "You're all so important to me, this season especially," I said. "Thank you for your work and selflessness."

Haley Puddy, a senior captain, raised her hand.

"Yes, Haley?"

"Coach Roos, we are doing this for Annabelle. We will do everything we can to win for her this weekend."

I willed my eyes to stay dry. "Thank you all. I appreciate that," I said. And then as usual, and to my relief, Josh punctured the sentiment, this time with "Who wants to explore this place?"

The girls fanned out, and with Jonas and the team moms still to come, I had a rare moment for something I'd attempted in the past months and never quite managed. Friends had suggested therapy, meditation,

> "Coach Roos, we are doing this for Annabelle. We will do everything we can to win for her this weekend."

retreats . . . but my default is activity. I'd write on a list to myself to call a therapist, and then I'd find a distraction. Before I could get into my bedroom, a load of laundry or social media would call my name. On this November day of 50 warm degrees, I lowered my solitary self into a lounge chair by the lake, laid my jacket over me as a blanket, and watched the slow waves touch the shore. Tree branches in the shallow water silhouetted against the horizon. I eased into my daily prayer: "Lord, let your will be done, whatever it is for this precious baby girl. I pray she will change lives and serve a purpose, whatever it is."

Lately Annabelle had been kicking, and as I prayed, she belted me. "Atta girl, Annabelle." I knew her as a fighter, no matter the score when she came into the game. The sun lowered and I thought about a *Jesus Calling* devotional from a few months earlier. *Do not worry about tomorrow! This is not a suggestion but a command. Your time divides into days and nights to help you handle life in manageable portions.*

Manageable portions. As in volleyball, to stay in the game, this pain with my name on it also needed timeouts.

A bit later Stacy Puddy, a team mom, met me in the terminal-sized kitchen to review the weekend menu: pasta for semifinals-eve dinner and breakfast tacos in the morning. Stacy had two daughters on the team, and she knew me well.

"Roos, ready to win another state championship?"

"Always ready."

Long look. "You doing all right?"

This was language to give me an out, but no brave face was necessary. "I think so," I said. She nodded, and I helped her unpack grocery bags and organize snacks. In a few minutes our Texas Catholic buddies rolled in, predictably wide-eyed.

"Tricia!" Jenna screamed. "You have got to be kidding me!"

"Welcome to my lake house!" I proclaimed, sweeping my arm. "Make yourselves comfortable!" Seth's eyes lit up, scanning, always scanning, for longshots and closeups. Our two reporters pulled out their gear, clipped a mic to my collar, and headed in to join us for dinner.

The aroma of pasta tripped sensors in our players' brains to crowd into the kitchen with healthy appetites. Anyone who believes teenage girls are delicate or indifferent eaters would lose that impression with my team. Tonight, they worked down a buffet line, sat full plates around a Texas-sized dining table, and waited for group prayer, which I led, thanking God for the playoff opportunity and for the astonishing roof over our heads. I asked for peace and rest that night, and someone threw in a stage whisper for a win. For us to all share a table was symbolically perfect. I would have liked to freeze frame on this scene, too; down the room Jenna and Seth quietly snapped pictures and shot footage.

Sports had taught me the practice of visualization, and in recent years I'd created a team tradition specific to volleyball for us that night and useful in life. One day soon it would serve me in Annabelle's birth. After dinner the girls gathered with blankets and pillows in a large upstairs living area. Most of them knew what was coming, but a few were novices.

"Everyone get to a comfortable spot," I said. "Lights out in two minutes," and they found places. When every girl seemed to be settled and quiet, I switched off the overheads.

"What in the world?" a freshman named Madi said, and her teammates laughed.

"Ladies," I said, "we are entering the mind gym. Through the next thirty minutes, we will walk through tomorrow's entire match. You will feel the AC on your arms, see the bright fluorescent lights, and hear cheers around you."

I'm a sports psychology nerd, and I wanted our players ready for everything ahead. We walked through the match, point for point, every moment an appeal to multiple senses. The squeak of shoes on a gym floor. The tang of the ball against their hands. The blur of faces in the stands. I described lasered shots and painful misses. Before it was over every girl would be called on to describe her feelings in a given moment. At the close, I announced our win, and the room erupted.

"That was so intense!" a junior exclaimed. "I could feel my heart in my chest the whole time!" Ready now, body and mind, our players headed to bed.

The next morning twenty-one players and managers wandered downstairs to the sounds and smells of team moms cooking bacon and eggs for breakfast tacos, our dietary sendoff before we loaded into the bus to the Corsicana High School gym. Inside the school, the head of TAPPS directed us to our locker room, and I peeled off to the bleachers to see the match before ours. One of my favorite pastimes is seeing winners at their winning moment, though it breaks my heart for any team to play its best and still lose. Whatever I did for Annabelle, I would lose her, I reasoned. Right then she made herself known in my stomach—a response to the noise and electricity around us.

When our team warm up began, I saw lightning in my players'

eyes—few words, but electricity shooting out fingertips. Antonian Preparatory was undefeated in its district. The school had multiple state championships. Their warmup attested to their confidence coming in, but their glances across the net did nothing to affirm it.

The game commenced and our team pocketed the lead. We never looked back, and my blood pressure hovered in range. My team knew of my doctor's warnings. The best over-the-counter preventive, I told them, was their 100 percent effort at all times. Our talent outshone any opposition, but when all the teams are talented, the battle is won on passion and effort. Capping the third set, our match point released a dogpile in midcourt. Bishop Lynch parents bounced in the stands. Tomorrow we'd play for the state title.

Back at the great house our nightly schedule hit replay: dinner, visualization, early lights out. The next day would bring Ursuline Academy, our crosstown foe of two matches this season already, and two wins for us. But a three-peat is no picnic, and the match could raise or lower our performance. I worked to keep the atmosphere light, made easier by Cameron and Jonas's joining us at the lake house. Cameron, a natural clown, hung out with the girls, who were rock stars in his eyes. By nine o'clock, the house was silent, and I was in prayer: *Protect Annabelle, and thy will be done.*

Then I heard myself ask God for victory, forcing me to reconsider and begin again, praying this time for my team and his will. *Help us to play our best and compete, but no matter the outcome, I will praise and worship you for this exceptional season.* I wanted God's will more than my win. As with my pregnancy, my job was to love his plan vs. pushing for my own. That night I must have fallen right to sleep.

This time I met the morning on edge, keenly aware that the girls felt the same. Today we'd have a few hours to wait before our match. Busloads of Bishop Lynch students would be in the stands, upping the excitement and pressure. Before we headed out for the gym, I met briefly with my captains.

"How's everyone?" I asked, and saw each girl wordlessly nominate someone else to speak.

"Nervous," they said, almost in unison.

"I get that, but you've played Ursuline. You guys are ready for this."

More glances. "What else?" I said.

Sofia spoke. "We don't want to lose for you . . . or for Annabelle." Ahh. I'd never wanted my pregnancy to add to their pressure. It was hard enough to go undefeated into a state championship.

"I'm glad you shared that with me," I said. "I know your dedication for yourselves and for me, but you can do nothing to disappoint me or her. We've had an amazing season. You've all gotten me through the hardest time of my life. Make sure the team knows that."

They looked relieved, these captains, three of the most mature teenagers I'd had the privilege of working with, and I cherished their candor.

The team packed to leave our fairytale housing. I walked back to the water to tell God again that I knew I was abundantly blessed. Annabelle was still alive inside of me. Exceptional young women had helped me survive four tenuous months. Now they'd give their all to honor Annabelle, but more than wins, they had turned my pain to joy. Starting tomorrow, my focus would shift to my birth plan. I looked at my watch, took a deep breath and headed for the bus. Win or lose, today was about the team I loved.

To hit their warmup in high form, in the locker room the girls jacked up music to dance and jump and break a sweat. While they did that, as I had the day before, I watched the match preceding ours. To qualify for the state game is one brand of excitement. To score the championship is priceless, and I believed that could be us. Annabelle tumbled in me like a flat tire on a moving car. Surely everyone in the bleachers could see the heel of her foot sweeping back and forth across my belly. I wore a tight maternity short-sleeve black shirt over a long black-and-white skirt—our school colors—in a fashion tradition that maternity clothes made harder to keep. Officials blew the take-the-court whistle. *Thy will be done.* Playing the Ursuline Bears, our tradition is to wear bear-hunt camouflage. In the stands today, however, I also saw hundreds of "Annabelle's Army" shirts, and the anxiety in me gave way to a smile.

The match began, and we were out of sync. Disjoint communication between my players was causing beginner's mistakes. I broke in with timeouts. Near the end of the first set our focus seemed back on track, but the set went to Ursuline. Their crowd went wild, and our fans looked stunned. I exchanged a look with my dad, who never missed a game.

"We're fine," Josh said to me. "We're better than they are. We just need to remember and believe it."

The girls formed a tight huddle, arms entwined, waiting for me to submit the lineup to the officials and join them. Inside the circle, I made eye contact with every player. "Ladies," I said, "today is about being in the moment and doing what you love. Worry about one point at a time and support each other. You'll be fine." Another glance around the circle to see head nods and confidence return. Through a long season they had pressed into every challenge. No giving up now.

With the start of the second set, the energy shifted, and so did the score. We took set two, then set three, up two to one, with the championship in view. Inside me Annabelle kicked like a Rockette, as if the match in her honor would not find her on the sidelines. In set four we took early control and sealed victory with a resounding shot by one of my star players. Fans and parents shot up in the stands like Fourth of July fireworks; the court was a dog pile of bodies and emotions. That the girls had made the effort for Annabelle seared into me.

The match ended late, but before heading home we found a local Chili's for a celebratory team dessert. Cameron moved slyly from table to table, sampling every player's order. Then it was back to Dallas.

CHAPTER 17

REALITY

SOMETIME AFTER MIDNIGHT Cameron woke and vomited every bite of every dessert from the evening before—effectively a bucket of ice water over my head after our victory. *Earth to Tricia: You're back.* We put Cameron in our bed and in the morning kept him home from church.

That week brought the dreaded second appointment at the Fetal Care Center, which I knew would leave me feeling worse for the visit. Per Dr. Martin, however, I'd requested the male doctor in the practice. Jonas and I waited in the cave-like sonogram room, resolved to at least give him a fair shake.

"Dr. Magee will be here shortly," a new nurse informed us. I glanced at Jonas.

"It's all good," he said. "Dr. Martin said he's much nicer, right?"

"If he's not, I'll throw a fit. They need to accept that we are staying with this pregnancy," I said. With my goodwill missing in action, I was reviewing where I might have left it when the door opened and a tall man in his mid-fifties brought in a large smile.

"You must be Mr. and Mrs. Roos," he said, shaking hands with both of us. "I'm Dr. Magee, and I'm honored to work with you. Shall we get started?"

On that impression alone, I began to mentally draft a thank you to Dr. Martin. The next plus was when our sonogram came onto the screen with no sad looks from the doctor—no sighs or side-eye. With a hand on the wand on my stomach and a hand tapping his computer, he measured Annabelle and hummed. He made a final note, and then he looked up and said, "Wanna play a little game with her?"

"A what?"

"It's fun."

I felt myself smile. "Sure," I said, "but what do you play with a baby in the womb?"

"Watch me," he said. With his finger he pressed my belly near where we knew Annabelle's head was. On the screen, a cloud appeared near her tiny face. Her hands flew up as if to wave it off.

My jaw dropped. "That is so cool!" I said. "How did you know she would do that?"

"It's what they do," he said laughing. "You try it."

Jonas and I played with Annabelle, no longer a floating pea but a small person with features that I recognized and loved. I shuddered to think what we might have missed by shutting down this session. She was our daughter, and this doctor made our time with her joyful, even extended, letting us play first with 3-D sonograms and then 4-D, effectively a video in real time.

"Dr. Magee," I said at last, probably because I'd feared asking sooner, "do you see changes or progress with Annabelle?" He paused, my cue to brace for the truth.

"No positive changes, unfortunately," he said. "I encourage you to enjoy every moment with her, and leave this in God's hands. I can tell you what I see, but it won't affect your plans."

This need-to-know approach I could accept. "Do you think I will make it full term?" I said.

"You're at about 32 weeks right now?"

"Correct."

"Well, anything is possible," he said. "You've made it this long, so I think you *can* make it to full term, but it's unlikely. You need to prepare for anything."

Even tough news from a doctor who cared was welcome now, and we left with a photo album of Annabelle. Outside, leaves were turning, and temperatures were cooling. My life had narrowed to taking each day for what it was. Crying dominated my morning commutes. At work I held back the tears mostly. At night I often cried myself to sleep. I tried to pray, to understand, to see the bigger picture and find courage, but most often the best I could manage was more tears. Volleyball was gone, and my swollen ankles made walking difficult.

One day in week thirty-six, Jonas and I met at Baylor Hospital with the head of NICU and the unit's doctors and nurses. Annabelle's arrival, when it came, would require a plan to cover every possibility. From our house we drove west to downtown Dallas, parked in the hospital garage, and followed the signs to "Labor & Delivery." Down a hall lined in black-and-white portraits of adorable babies, as if in an out-of-body experience, I waddled to the muffled sounds of crying newborns. When Annabelle came, this would be the hallway to our delivery room. Jonas and I reached the elevators, rode two floors up, and waited as the doors opened.

"You must be Tricia and Jonas!" a smiling nurse said, greeting us at the door. Seeming to need no confirmation, she leaned in to hug me.

"I am," I said, leaving the elevator and returning the hug. "I'm Tricia and you must be Julie."

"Julie Crawford," she said. "An honor to meet you both." She led us to the room where our NICU team stood up to give us the greeting I'd come to expect: gentle smiles, sincere handshakes, and sad eyes.

"Tricia and Jonas, thank you for coming," said a tall man in a lab coat. "If you'll have a seat, we'll introduce you to your hospital delivery team." Jonas and I found a small couch and sat down.

For deliveries of premature babies or babies with health issues, these seasoned professionals were a dream team of towering medical degrees. As the meeting progressed, however, hearing no mention of Trisomy 18, I had a question.

"Excuse me," I said, "but before we go further . . ."

"Ask us anything," Julie said.

"Has anyone here ever delivered a baby with Trisomy 18?"

Silence. Like the captains on my team, every doctor and nurse seemed to want someone else to respond. The quiet grew uneasy. At last an older doctor said, "No, Mrs. Roos, we have not delivered a live Trisomy 18 birth at this hospital, not since any of us have worked here."

The sad eyes at our greeting took on new meaning. They weren't sad just for my situation. They were sad because my medical team held no chance of survival for my daughter. I was stunned, and I cleared my throat to buy time. "No disrespect," I said, "but am I at the right place? Is there another hospital that might have more experience or specialize in handling children with Trisomy 18?"

Julie again. "Unfortunately, Tricia, no hospitals in this area have delivered babies with Trisomy 18 because live births are so rare. We can promise that we will take the best care of you and your daughter, no matter what happens."

It wasn't the answer I wanted, but it was sincere, and the staff's expertise was still considerable. Our talk returned to the birth plan, and to hard questions to help prepare the NICU staff to act on our wishes. Julie produced sample birth plans to help us create a written version for the day of delivery, when every doctor and nurse caring for us would have a copy. This is what I kept putting off: what level of care to give Annabelle if she survived birth in extreme stress or pain. The options were so wide-ranging. I suppose I'd thought the doctors would know what to do, but that would not be our finish line.

Fifteen years before when my grandfather died, he'd had a stroke and declined quickly. My grandmother, my dad and his brother had to decide whether to put him on a ventilator and if so, for how long. I'd had no appreciation for what that put them through. This responsibility now for my daughter's survival overwhelmed me.

The meeting ended, and we stood to leave. Julie took my arm. "We'll get through this," she said, looking me in the eye. "I will help you every step of the way." I could only nod. I sensed her faith in God, and I trusted her.

We left the meeting and returned to a world decked out for the holidays, the birth of Jesus. But all I could see was cold and rain, a mirror of the gray fear taking me over. All my life I had loved Christmas. Now a three-year-old in our house loved it as much as I had—the tree and decorations, the songs, and, his chief priority, the gifts—but those things belonged now to a world closed off to me.

Before the break, Bishop Lynch celebrates an all-school Mass. This year I had no heart for it because church always brought the risk of a public meltdown. Every song, every message, undid me, and I had exhausted my reserves.

After the last class of the last day, putting one foot in front of the other, I made myself walk to the competition gym and find a seat among the senior students. Underclassmen filled the bleachers, but by now I could only endure chairs with backs. The priest spoke about Mary just before she gave birth to Jesus. In her difficulties—worn from the arduous journey to Bethlehem, no places to stop and rest—she accepted God's plan for her life, and that was enough.

Though I sat among more than a thousand people, the priest spoke to me alone. As in my dream months before, I was being told to hold to my faith, nothing more. I was not giving birth to our Savior, but in Mary's faith I had a path to Annabelle's birth. By the end of Mass, I had traded fear for faith and my worries for God's promises. Hard times lay ahead, but if I could see through Mary's eyes, I could stay in God's plan and choose for Annabelle within his will.

CHAPTER 18

CHRISTMAS

———————

THE FINAL MONTH of pregnancy typically is marked by misery, but my final month set new lows. For starters, Annabelle's inability to swallow amniotic fluid—the part of her condition that made her unnaturally small—made me catastrophically large.

And woefully sensitive. Wobbling into the waiting room for my thirty-eight-week appointment I felt women's eyes leave their magazines and phones to stare. From strangers I could take it, but coming from mothers in this waiting room, every look cut.

Putting salt in the wound, Christmas decorations lined the waiting area, and the receptionist wore a Santa hat. "Good afternoon, Mrs. Roos. Just sign in," she said cheerily. "And do you have a sonogram appointment today?"

I nodded. "Yes," I said. I found a nearby chair and lowered myself into it. Hearing my name, Jonas and I took the worn route downstairs, each slow step a new threat to my skewed center of gravity.

"Let's see what little Annabelle is doing in there today," Janet said in the sonogram room. By now she and the office staff felt like personal friends, not just to me but on Annabelle's behalf. To my joy they spoke of her by name. Jonas and I had chosen it with care, and we let people know why. Our daughter was a person, a human being. It mattered to us that the people in our lives acknowledge her.

Now from where I lay on my back, I had a direct view to Janet's eyes and the looks of concern on her face.

"Tricia, so much fluid. Has Dr. Martin talked to you?"

"We talked about it," I said. "It feels like there's a lot more in just the last few days."

Her wand ran up and down, she hit "print," and then she pressed my hand. "I don't know if I'll see you again before you give birth," she said gravely. "Good luck to you guys, and God bless."

I couldn't speak, so Jonas said thank you. I buttoned up my shirt and we headed upstairs, where Dr. Martin stood with a giant file that included that day's sonogram. Whatever was imminent, I prayed to do what was best for Annabelle.

"We need to schedule the C-section immediately," Dr. Martin said. "The images show an incredible amount of fluid. This can quickly get dangerous for you *and* Annabelle."

Whatever my face did, when she saw it her voice softened. "You made it this far, Tricia," she said. "A full term, technically, is thirty-seven weeks. Waiting too long with this polyhydramnios—this amniotic fluid build-up—-could affect our meeting her alive."

Until now everything I'd read or researched said the baby's time in the womb affects her chance of survival. Though, true, none of the reports factored in fluid buildup.

"So, when you say C-section as soon as possible,'" I said slowly, "when would that be?"

She held a calendar. My original due date was January 5; this was the last week of December. "Today is Tuesday and Christmas is on Thursday. How about I clear my schedule and we have her next Monday, December 29th?" she said. "I'm out over New Year's and, honestly, I don't want anyone else doing this."

"Okay to December 29," I said, reaching for Jonas's arm. That much made sense. "What now?"

"My nurse will check with the hospital to coordinate with several folks there," she said. "We'll try to confirm tomorrow before everyone takes off for Christmas."

So, it was real. For eight months I'd believed that somehow with Annabelle inside me I could keep her safe. The outside world was always her battleground, and now her one-sided fight had a date. My courage from the Christmas Mass at school felt faint and far away. How many times had people told me God gave me Annabelle because he knew I could handle it? Could I? No. I could not. What if she lost ground after birth? How could I make rational decisions on her behalf? The more I analyzed, the more I dreaded; the more I dreaded, the worse I felt.

> The outside world was always her battleground, and now her one-sided fight had a date.

That night, like so many, I fell asleep in tears, this time waking at six o'clock to Cameron's shouts from the side of our bed. "Mommy! Daddy! It's Swedish Christmas!" He plunged under the covers and wedged himself to cuddle my belly. "Annabelle!" he whispered, "I bet you get some presents from Santa!"

Sweden celebrates Christmas on Christmas Eve—a big gift to the Roos family in the US in terms of how we schedule time with our families. "Long-distance Sweden" was the morning of the 24th; the afternoon we spent with Jonas's mom and stepdad in Frisco, forty-five minutes north. Christmas cheer seemed in short supply, but Cameron's three-year-old wonder was getting us a long way.

This year he'd mastered the concepts of Santa, chimneys, presents, and the bonus in his binational roots. After the morning online with Mormor and Farmor, who were outside Stockholm, we drove to Frisco. Within seconds of a hug and a kiss from his

Dallas Farmor, Cameron was in the living room under the extra-tall Christmas tree, looking for his name on gift tags.

Lena and Keith's open-concept apartment with its floor-to-ceiling windows turn a thousand square feet into a home in the clouds—topped that day only by Lena's decorations and cooking, which ease Christmas duties for everyone else. We walked into the aroma of ham in the oven.

"Let me get you something to drink," Keith said.

"I'll take a scotch and water," I said, and Keith—my partner in banter and sarcasm—burst into laughter. Like me, Keith indulges in movie quotes, chief among them almost any line from *Dumb & Dumber* and *Wayne's World*. A person had to admire his love of the classics. "Hold the scotch," I said, to complete the quote from *The Waterboy*.

Keith's son, who was my age, had died a few years earlier in a car accident, and Keith had survived on faith alone. These days he kept our conversations light, I believe, because he knew so much. Seeing Cameron under the tree, the adults delayed dinner to let him tear into a few gifts after so many weeks of having to wait.

Waiting was my strong suit. I longed to hold Annabelle, but the price of that moment tied me in knots. Early in my pregnancy I'd read that coral reefs live and thrive in the ocean, but out of the water, they immediately begin to die, and the picture haunted me. Expert after expert warned us that Annabelle, with her two-chamber heart and tiny body, most likely would be stillborn. I struggled to prepare myself to meet my child after she was already gone.

At some point in these months of unknowing, I had looked at a Facebook group for Trisomy 18 parents. Pictures of stillbirths appeared next to love letters from the parents, where the joy of birth met the agony of loss. A year ago, who would have guessed that I would understand those parents so well.

Christmas dinner in Frisco was easy and warm. The next week was on all our minds, but we concentrated on being together.

Cameron played with his remote-control car and superhero figures, the sun lowered, and we headed for Christmas Eve at our church.

Sunday mornings we attend a contemporary service with a band and stage. Christmas Eve, in contrast, is one candlelight service for everyone, in the great sanctuary, always ending in *Silent Night* acapella. I made it through the carols and readings, but as hundreds of candles became starry points of light, and the world held its breath, I felt the weight of the life and death facing me, and I wept. I thought of my dream and of Annabelle's funeral in this place. Because of Jesus' death, she would be whole and with him. "Thank you," I whispered, one hand on my belly, one hand holding a light.

My C-section was scheduled for Monday evening at five o'clock. The weekend before was a frenzy of putting Christmas decorations back in storage and cleaning the house. Nesting is a proven phenomenon among pregnant women, and here I was in the statistical median. However slim the chances of bringing home our special baby, if a chance existed, her home would be ready. Depending on a future impossible to know, her hospital stay, if there was one, could be days or weeks. My side of the family had given me newborn onesies that would turn out to be too big, but I packed them for the hospital next to clothes for me.

As for Cameron, the boy who believed, that weekend he and his parents spent extra hours together. At various times we told him Jesus might bring his sister back to heaven to fix her heart, but it was water on a duck's back. With everything in him, Cameron knew Annabelle was coming to stay.

Two

A WISH IN TIME

DAY ONE

DECEMBER 29

GIVING BIRTH BY going into labor as opposed to a C-section is the difference between running back-to-back marathons and catching a ride to the finish line. Before Jonas took me to the hospital to have Annabelle by C-section, I kept a hair appointment, fit in a pedicure, and still had room in the day for Jonas and me to spend time with family. True, with the swelling and fluid retention I looked like Violet in *Charlie and the Chocolate Factory* after she blows up into a giant blueberry, but if the surgery room was full of observers, at least my hair and nails wouldn't embarrass me.

The highpoint was the pedicure, when I could pay a professional to massage my swollen feet. That day I used the time to close my eyes and think through the year of the pregnancy that had become a chain of blindsides. Twelve months before, almost to the day, Jonas and I had been at the Fiesta Bowl in Arizona cheering for Baylor University, enjoying a warm escape from a cold month in Texas. On New Year's Eve, we'd crowded into a noisy bar with our friends, and I'd prayed as the ball dropped that 2014 would bring our next child.

The answer that came continued to change our faith, our marriage, our relationships—and I regretted nothing.

That afternoon of the C-section, Jonas and I reviewed plans with my sister, April, close to me in age, and so close in looks that some of my team moms mixed us up. April is the top candidate in any enterprise for COO; now she was in charge of updates to our family and friends. Text chains and phone conversations were impossible for me, obviously, but those speed bumps April cleared handily with "Annabelle's Army," a Facebook page that soon became its own story . . . And then—*whoa, time to go.* Time to take every moment on its own, no borrowing from the next day or even the next hour.

At Baylor Hospital in downtown Dallas our elevator door pulled open at the maternity floor. We signed in, and I was led to a prep room to change into a surgery gown. A nurse hooked me to an IV and a heart-rate monitor.

"Tricia?" Our NICU nurse, Julie, walked in. "We're so excited you're here! Everyone is getting ready for you. This is Dr. York, your neonatologist."

A petite blonde in a lab coat shook my hand. "Good to meet you, Tricia." This was the two-woman team to help me determine at birth, moment by moment, how to care for Annabelle, wanting now to review our game plan. This very minute. Fair enough—I knew in my mind—but as I agreed to it, my arms and legs began to shake.

Julie handed us copies of my file, and the three of us reviewed every scenario for Annabelle's first minutes post birth. Even if she should survive, no two-chamber heart would last for long. In every case, Jonas and I wanted her basic needs provided for—attention any baby would receive. No heart surgery, no respirator or extreme measures, but standard care. Most of the questions for me today covered possible interventions, at what points the doctors would step in and to what degree. Jonas and I said nothing should give Annabelle pain, nothing should prevent my holding her. Earlier in my pregnancy, I'd had a mental picture of her dying, her body a pin cushion of tubes as she lay isolated in an incubator. That would not happen. At the same time, if an intervention could ease a problem without causing pain, we were for it.

The medical term is "comfort intervention." If Annabelle struggled for breath, yes to oxygen. If her mouth could be suctioned to avoid choking, yes. On paper, the decisions looked right enough, but birth details also made death real, and suddenly no amount of blankets could stop my shaking. Maybe this was more than a panic attack, I thought. Maybe it was a mental breakdown. Like a car hitting black ice, I had spun into second guessing when calm entered the room in the person of Sam Holm, our church's associate pastor.

"How are you?" he asked simply, coming to where I lay on a rollaway bed. "Is it all right if I pray with you?" I nodded and my tears—always the tears—streamed. He prayed, I closed my eyes, and like entering the mental gym before a big game, I felt peace and confidence flow in. I was in the zone, aware of sights and sounds and smells, narrowing every thought to my breaths, to Annabelle in me, to a psalm of positive reminders. *I know I will see her. I know I will meet her. I know she will be alive. I trust my doctors. I believe God has a plan for Annabelle.*

In the distance I heard Sam say amen but I stayed in my mental safe room. My C-section with Cameron had been unscheduled, an emergency, in and out. Now I was hearing that any emergency C-section would preempt mine. Our 5 p.m. delivery was delayed repeatedly for what felt like hours. But it was one hour, and I stayed in the mental gym, and at last my bed was moving down a hall. A cool breeze passed over my arms and upper body. Below my stomach I felt nothing, compliments of my epidural. Now from drugs or shock, my thoughts began to fog and I strained to stay present for Annabelle's birth. My bed entered an operating room of blinding lights with a forest of moving figures, and my acuity inched back. My body was moved to a table, and there was Dr. Martin, head-to-toe in scrubs, gloves, goggles and mask.

"Ready to do this?" she said. Her voice sounded normal and upbeat.

"I am," I said. "Please be careful with her."

A nurse drew a curtain across my stomach. Jonas found my hand. For months the weight against my organs when I laid on my back had been bad for the baby and excruciating for me. Now I was back in the pain position, struggling for a deep breath, pleading silently to endure. And then, as if a hand had pulled a plug, the pressure in me drained away.

"Is Annabelle out?" I asked. From the other side of the curtain, Dr. Martin laughed. "That's your fluid, Tricia," she said. "You retained about two gallons." Aware of the observers in the room, I was mortified. I heard the sound of liquid draining. I stared at the ceiling, anxious, restless. Dr. Martin's safety steps slowed the time to a crawl.

Then I heard her say "almost there." And then she said, "One more layer and she's out." I strained for every update. An uncomfortable weight pulled against my skin. "I'm bringing her out," Dr. Martin was saying. "Okay, I'm holding her in my arms. I'm passing her to the nurses."

My heart thundered. "Is she okay?" I shouted. "Is she alive?" Why was no one answering me? I fixed on Jonas's face, trying to read the room in his eyes, when Julie appeared at my side.

"Tricia, she's not breathing; she's blue," Julie said. More commotion. More noise.

A nurse shouted, "She's breathing! We're working on her! We'll get her to you right away!"

And then, like the purr of a lion cub, a soft cry reached my ears. On either side of me, my fists slackened. My child was coming to me. A doctor directed Jonas as he gingerly laid a doll-sized figure near where my shoulder met my neck. "Kangaroo care," they call it, skin-to-skin contact with the mother to regulate the newborn's vitals. To the right of my face, I could make out tiny cheeks and a spindly body a coral shade of pink. So gently Jonas pressed her to me. If I couldn't have her in my arms, I could feel her entirety. After too many long months, our little Annabelle's heart was beating. She was alive, and she was with us.

Someone said "17.5 inches" — *long!* —and then "3 lbs., 13 oz.," and Jonas's gaze met mine. "She's so small," he said, as if fearing to touch such a diminutive being.

"She's alive and she's perfect," I murmured. I angled my head. My daughter's perfectly round little face fed my gaze, and I loved her. All the people who should know had said this was impossible, but we'd prayed for it. And here was our answer, clearly ours, one-hundred percent Roos with Cameron's little nose. Like most newborns, her eyes were bright blue. In a few minutes more my stomach was sewn back together, and my gurney was moving to recovery. I was nauseous from the drugs.

What a wretched thing to throw up just after your stomach has been cut open. After Cameron's delivery, on the elevator ride to my hospital room, I had all but hurled him into a nurse's arms to avoid baptizing him with my stomach lining. The same vertigo was back.

"Ma'am, I don't feel . . ." I said to a nurse. "I think I'm going to . . ."

"No, you are not," she snapped. "You will spend every second with your baby. I'll get something in your IV," and in a few minutes the nausea receded.

Now we were in the recovery room, normally for immediate family only, but Baylor had set up a larger space for Annabelle to meet her people. As our longed-for miracle lay on my chest, like a Noah's ark procession, family members approached in twos and threes. Every possible feeling flowed through me, but uppermost I felt content, in a haze of love.

Annabelle's fairy-light heart rate held steady as long as our bodies held close, and there we stayed. At some point a clock said only 7:00 p.m., but I could swear I'd been on the Six Flags Spinsanity ride for most of the day. Now everything in me craved quiet with my daughter and husband, and our nurses read my mind. They cleared the receiving area and moved us to our room, where family members took turns telling Annabelle goodnight. For forever? No one knew. For now, for hours, in a cloud of serenity, Jonas and I lay holding our girl.

By hospital protocol, a newborn with special needs stays in NICU for round-the-clock care, and the mother visits. In our case, the NICU arranged our room to keep us together there. Through the long night watch, people in white coats and scrubs entered and left while my body rejected sleep. Hour by hour I took in my child's familiar and precious features, alert to any signs of short or irregular breathing. And so passed our first night together.

DAY TWO

DECEMBER 30

FOR NEWBORNS UNABLE to swallow, the standard procedure is to run a feeding tube through the baby's nose to her stomach. On Annabelle's first morning of life our doctors warned us that a tube could put her at high risk of aspiration—the accidental breathing in of food or fluid—and so we held off. If getting nutrients into Annabelle might kill her, and because no one ever anticipated her living even this long, if she was calm and content, we'd take no chances.

Every quarter hour seemed to bring another high-risk decision. The next was who could hold Annabelle, as strange as that sounds, and we kept the circle small. In a hospital room filled to maximum capacity with family and friends, she went from her dad's chest to April's arms and back to my chest. With any change in breathing, she was back on me to hit reset. For hours I stroked her tiny head of soft, fuzzy brown hair, whispering to her who was there and how she knew them.

The talk of the room was her response to Cameron. Most of the time she lay on my chest, her eyes closed, softly purring. But when a certain boy came near and spoke to her, with her right eye pressed to me, her left eye would peek open and her neck raise slightly as she tried to turn to him.

"Hello, my sweet sister Annabelle," Cameron would say in his new "Big Brother" shirt and gently pat her. Then he'd exclaim, "She did it again, Mom! She opened her eye to look at me when I said her name!"

"I know it, buddy. She loves her big brother," Jonas would say. "She wants to see you."

The intensity drained us all. By midafternoon the adults around us looked like war refugees, and Cameron needed a field to run in. April in particular, seventeen weeks pregnant, was withering. Jonas thanked our beloved first-string supporters and sent them all home, a line forming again to kiss Annabelle goodnight. In a few minutes silence reigned again, and gratitude flooded in.

Was all this real? Annabelle's two-chamber heart was made to fail, everyone said so. But she seemed to be in the business of busting probabilities. April reported thousands of hits on the "Annabelle's Army" page, and we felt the prayers. How awareness of her had boomed, and so quickly, was another miracle. Now with our hospital room down to three souls, Jonas stood and stretched.

"Want anything from the cafeteria?" he asked me. For thirty-six hours now, he'd been with me every minute, awake and in the room.

"I think I'm good, but you get something," I said. "Get some snacks for later."

A NICU nurse came in. "How is our girl?" she said. I arched my neck to get a view of Annabelle's little face.

"From time to time her breathing is labored," I said, "but she's happy."

The nurse had caught the end of the talk about the cafeteria, and she waved Jonas on. "Take a break," she urged him. "I'll hang with Tricia and Annabelle."

"Go," I repeated. "We'll be fine." Jonas disappeared into the hall. At the end of my bed the nurse began to input notes on the computer.

"May I hold her for a few minutes to check her heart rate?" she asked me. Reluctantly I let her lift Annabelle up and away from my chest. From where I lay on my back, I watched her slowly, carefully turn our little bundle over. Off came the pink monogrammed blanket that swaddled her and the preemie onesie hanging on her birdlike frame. Annabelle was at my feet, her tiny chest rising and falling, when the nurse returned to her work on the computer.

I stared for a beat. "Wait!" I shouted. "Stop! She's not breathing!"

The nurse's head whipped back to the bed, her eyes wide. She picked up Annabelle and held her upright, but nothing. I grabbed my phone. Jonas answered on the first ring.

"Get here now! She's not breathing!!" I shouted. The nurse held Annabelle's tiny body and my instincts exploded. "Put her on my chest!" I demanded. "Hand her to me! Hand her to me!" She laid Annabelle on my chest and began to massage her legs, her arms, her inches-long torso.

"Do it with me," the nurse instructed, and then Jonas was there.

"I don't know what happened," I said, almost wailing. "She was lying on her back, and then she wasn't breathing."

The nurse looked up at us. "She's breathing. It's okay." she said. "I can tell she's breathing again," and I began to sob.

Jonas wrapped his arms around Annabelle and me. The nurse stepped back, her face white. Clinically, we knew to expect scares, but the reality hit hard, and more lay ahead. Apnea, the nurse called it, when Annabelle's little system failed to tell her body to breathe. Deep sleep made her especially susceptible. The nurse's massage was to stimulate Annabelle's nerves, reminding her to take a breath.

"She seems to be stable now, but if it happens again, call us. We'll be here as soon as we can," the nurse said, and I felt sorry for her.

"Thank you for getting Annabelle back to us," I murmured, and then she was gone. Jonas and I hugged and cried and gave in to exhaustion. To try to sleep, I rigged a kangaroo pouch, securing Annabelle's little body to my big one. Jonas flipped wall switches until the only light was the red glow of the heart-rate monitor. Lulled by its soft beep, I fell into a twilight state, part of me alert to the cadence of my child's breathing, part of me tangled in the stresses of her second day of life. Half conscious, I prayed for strength and endurance beyond my reach.

DAY THREE

DECEMBER 31

———

THROUGH THE NIGHT, the tempo of Annabelle's breathing came and went. By morning, she was in a fragile groove that we refused to disrupt. Every checkup, we said, *every one,* would be with her lying on me. And though the night had been a blur of blood pressure and heart-rate checks for Annabelle and pain medication for me, for her to still be with us made it Christmas morning again. Our family members drifted in, and we kept an ear out for the comic relief of Cameron's arrival. Jonas's parents were staying with him at our house, fifteen minutes from the hospital. I was updating Dad and April on the drama of the night before when Jonas took a phone call and his face fell.

"What? Is that your mom?" I said. He nodded and signaled for me to wait.

"All right. Keep us posted," he was saying, and he slid the phone into his front pocket. "Cameron has a fever and isn't feeling well," he reported. "Mom thinks he should stay home." My spirits sagged. Our exuberant little guy so seldom got sick; the few times he did, I wanted to hold him close. Jonas reminded me he was in good hands, and my father turned the talk to stories in the news. In a few minutes we were back in conversation, my hand lightly on Annabelle's back, sensitive to its rise and fall, when I felt her little frame go still.

I cried out, "She's not breathing! Call the nurse!"

The room was electrified. Jonas, my dad, and my sister bent over me. "Massage her body," I urged. "Her legs and arms and body!" In seconds a nurse took over. She pulled out her stethoscope and motioned for silence.

"It's okay, it's okay," she said. "She's breathing again."

Another faceoff with death, this time with the family in ringside seats. After that, every few hours brought more episodes, each one another drain on our hopes and on Annabelle's reserves. Medical personnel, meanwhile, repeated to us that she physically could not swallow, and that a feeding tube could kill her, and with deepening dread we watched our little girl lose ground. At six o'clock that evening the shift changed to possibly our final medical team. A new NICU nurse came in with a stack of charts.

> Another faceoff
> with death,
> this time with
> the family in
> ringside seats.

"I'm Shelley," she said, sounding the most positive tone of the day. "How's it been for our patient? My charts say she's had a rough go."

"Yeah, rough," I said wearily. "She can't swallow or take a feeding tube, so she's growing weaker. I don't see how she can last much longer."

Nurse Shelley considered my words. "You tried to feed her?"

"We tried a few times. We offered her my milk on a Q-Tip, but no luck."

"I'd like to give it another try," Shelley said. Glancing around, she picked up a plastic spoon, tore off its cellophane wrapper, and handed it to me.

"What do I do with this?" I asked, and she laughed.

"You put some of your milk on it, and we see if she'll take any."

I did my part, after which Shelley carefully took the spoon of liquid and dipped in a Q-Tip. She had me raise Annabelle higher on my chest for a better angle. Moving in close, she held the Q-Tip to Annabelle's tiny nose.

"If she can smell it, she may want to try it," Shelley explained—news to me, but I was on board. "Hey, sweet girl," she whispered. "Would you like something to eat?" She coated Annabelle's lips with my milk, paused a beat, then held the Q-Tip before her mouth. Tiny nostrils flared and a tiny body stirred.

"Come on, Annabelle," I said. "You can do it." Her lips parted, and she sucked on the Q-Tip. I rocketed up in bed. "I can't believe this!" I said. "She did it!"

Shelley grinned without looking up. "She sure did. Now let's see if she'll eat some more." We had the drill—nose then mouth—and with every taste, Annabelle sucked harder on the Q-Tip. Instead of preparing to see her die, through the miracle of our new night-shift nurse, we were seeing our little fairy return to life. Before long, sated and sleepy, Annabelle melted against my chest, her breathing even.

"Shelley," I said quietly. "We thought it was over."

With barely a pause she said, "Now to get you out of bed to walk a little bit. You have to take care of yourself too." Looking up to see my face, she added, "We're only going to the hall. We can bring Annabelle with us, or Jonas can hold her a bit."

Showing the grace and agility of a two-by-four, I shifted my body to the side of the bed, keenly aware that the longer I stayed inert, the more complicated my recovery. If Annabelle could eat, however, I could walk. Still holding her to my chest, I eased my feet over the bed and touched the floor, sending blood into my lower limbs, causing a howl from my lips that surprised even me. But I stayed up. I gave Annabelle to Shelley and, step by brutal step, made my way propped against Jonas. Like holding a carrot on a stick, Shelley pushed the crib ahead of us, my eyes glued to it.

"I'm watching her every breath," Shelley assured me in an afternoon-practice coaching voice. "You concentrate on walking."

When I was finally back at my bed, Jonas arranged my pillows. Shelley gently returned our little sparrow to her place between my shoulder and neck. "Now a bath," said the nurse with a two-for-two record of getting Roos to exceed expectations.

"Maybe not this minute," she said next, this time reading my mind. "I'll bring everything from the NICU, and we'll do it here together. We'll have a nice heating lamp to keep Annabelle toasty."

"If it's in here . . ." I said from the pillows. A Mary Poppins smile appeared on our nurse's face. "You two rest with Annabelle," she said to Jonas and me. "I'll be back in a little while."

How quickly the world and everything in it can change. Annabelle cooed in my arms, my milk was in her tummy, and her daddy dozed nearby. In an hour Shelley was back, wheeling in a clear plastic basin attached to a heating tower already emitting warmth.

"A little baby hot tub," I observed, and Jonas laughed from the couch.

"Any way I could fit in it?" he said wearily, and Shelley gave him a rain check. "We'll focus on Annabelle for today. Everyone ready to help?"

"Ready," I said. "Tell us what to do."

We undressed Annabelle and lifted her to the plastic basin. Cautiously, we took turns dipping her wiry little frame into the water. Shelley soaped a miniature washcloth and sudsed Annabelle's limbs in circular motions. As if on a visit to an earlier home, our daughter's whisper of a body relaxed into the familiar feel of fluid and warmth. I watched her, helpless, trusting us for even the air she breathed. I thought of our dependence on our medical staff.

If we hadn't known to massage her through the apnea episodes . . . if Shelley hadn't asked to try again. Seeing this precious little life at the mercy of our choices undid me. I took in the lavender scent, the glow of the lamp, the kiss of her days-old skin in my hands. By the time we'd dabbed her with a soft towel and dried her light brown hair, she was asleep. Swathed in her soft blanket, she nestled into her spot near my heart, and I asked Jonas to turn on the TV.

I know the rule that when the baby sleeps the mother sleeps, but tonight was New Year's Eve. I wanted to greet the year that no one expected my child to see. The countdown came, and the ball began its descent.

DAY FOUR

JANUARY 1

———

DING (PAUSE) DING (pause) DING (pause) DING . . . day three of Annabelle's life opened to the sounds of the text on my cell phone blowing up. The night before I'd written April about Annabelle's first milk and bath, but my sister had collapsed into bed as soon as she got home. Now she was catching up on the drama.

I worked the sleep out of my eyes and pushed hair off my face. My chest was sweaty where Annabelle had spent the night. A knock on the door roused Jonas on the couch, and a hospital employee wheeled in our first bona fide meal in days—pancakes, sausage, and fruit. For Annabelle's sake, and for my own energy, it was time to eat better.

"May I hold her?" Jonas asked me, coming to the bed—a silly question normally, but for us a conscious decision every time. I tucked in two twig-like arms and legs, cupped my hands under her, and carefully transferred Annabelle to her dad. Jonas unbuttoned his shirt to lay her on his chest and returned to the couch.

This was the man I'd had the foresight to marry—the one who joined his friends one day in a beach volleyball game at Baylor and had been on my side ever since. Through the strains of Annabelle's diagnosis, my pregnancy, and the many stresses of not knowing, when all I could see was pain, this was the protector who kept his head above water to guide the rest of us. I devoured breakfast, then April arrived eager for details of the night before and Shelley's life-giving interventions.

"Any news from Mom about Cameron?" Jonas said, and April's face clouded. "We talked about seven this morning," she said. "He still has a fever. Looks like a cold."

The day before, I'd grieved his absence. Now I was grateful for all he was missing. Annabelle had made it through the night, but her troubles, random and intense, were too much for a little boy. Our room filled again with family. Flowers and balloons continued to crown the windowsill. Medical personnel routinely flowed in and out. And then came the question, from across the room and out of the blue.

"How long do you get to stay here, Tricia?" my mom asked innocently. My eyes traveled to Jonas.

"I have no idea," I said.

Jonas said he didn't know. No expert we had talked to, in his or her wildest dreams, had expected Annabelle to live this long, much less to leave the hospital. When a nurse came in to take Annabelle's vitals, we asked her.

"Ma'am, can you tell us when we check out or what comes next?"

"I don't know," she said. "I'll get a doctor in here to review it with you."

In a few minutes a young physician on floor duty appeared with an armful of charts and little by way of exit information. When I asked him if we were there for as long as Annabelle needed medical attention, he adjusted his glasses. Then, as if relieved to see it, he flapped a page stapled to a folder.

"It says here you check out with your daughter tomorrow at noon," he said, and my stomach twisted. Three and a half years before, when it was time to take a healthy baby named Cameron home from the hospital, I'd thrown up, extending our stay by another hour. It's possible my reply to this young doctor now sounded tense, even insistent. *Wouldn't Annabelle need medical supplies?* I said. *And wouldn't Jonas and I need training to be home with her?* My checklist of concerns would fill a city phone book, but they were for a doctor close to our situation. I thanked this doctor, and he hesitated.

"May I tell you something?" he said. Everyone in the room leaned in.

"Sure. Of course," I said.

"In medical school we learned that Trisomy 18 is incompatible with life," he said frankly. "On top of that, I would have said any child with a two-chamber heart didn't have a chance. Your daughter is teaching us things we thought were impossible."

I studied the small figure on my chest. "Thank you for that," I said softly. "It means a lot to think this could help doctors and parents know how much more can happen."

In the next hours, Annabelle had small apnea episodes. Several times her breathing stopped, and when it did our world halted on its axis. She'd take a catchup gulp, resettle into her breathing pattern, freeing us to go back to ours. We began to recognize when she was ready to eat. Her sucking skills grew with every milky Q-Tip. By now the nurses from her first days—the ones who cried when they'd said goodbye—cried to see her still alive. Annabelle was rewriting the book on Trisomy 18.

And she ate. And she rested. And our fears of her episodes subsided, and more people held her. We knew our paradise of medical expertise had a shelf life, just not what we would do without it.

Around three o'clock that afternoon, an especially small woman in heels and a lab coat knocked on our door and came in, her voice crackling with authority. "I'm sorry about your situation Mr. and Mrs. Roos," she said. "By tomorrow at noon, you'll be checked out of the hospital to care for Annabelle at home." The news was expected, but it was still a shock to leave the only safety system we'd known. From the crude lumber of fear, I tried to assemble a question.

"How do we take care of her?" I said weakly. "Will we have rented equipment? Will a nurse stay with us at our house?"

We'd declined an incubator. We'd declined interventions like breathing tubes and IVs. But the nursing staff was always nearby to help us naturally, like using a suction tool to clear her throat so she didn't choke.

"No equipment or nurse," the doctor was telling us. "It's best for you to provide her comfort care until her passing," and for the first time, the words "comfort care" landed on us like a bludgeon. We wanted options to promote life while we could. I couldn't insert a feeding tube. If she needed oxygen, I'd need help to administer it.

Around the room faces looked stunned. I said, "I've seen attachments on the front of a baby's diaper so that if they stop breathing, an alarm goes off. Is that something you can get us?"

"And add to the stress you're already under," she said.

More stress? This was stress. How could she know what stressed me or what Annabelle needed?

"I think we're trying to say we'd like the device that alerts us if our child stops breathing," Jonas said. "We'd like to go home with anything that can help us help her when she struggles."

"I understand the outcome," I said defensively. "I don't want her to be in pain in the process." I pulled Annabelle closer.

"I can prescribe some oxygen for you and send you home with one of the suction machines," the doctor said. "That's the most we should do."

We'd gone to the experts. Now we relied on them. The odds on Annabelle's life were harsh, but she was our child. One day physicians would study her record-busting survival, but that didn't change our wanting to keep her as long as we could. "Yes, please," I said to the doctor. She scribbled on a notepad and said goodbye. No mention of a feeding tube, no feeding

> The odds on Annabelle's life were harsh, but she was our child.

plan—but if Annabelle could suck milk from the Q-Tip, for now we had that.

After dinner with family, the room again emptied except for April, always first to arrive and last to leave. When our parents' divorce had left certain relationships rocky, April was the buffer on all sides. When Jonas and I needed a break, she was my trusted assistant, as attentive to Annabelle as I was, and never off the job.

"A nurse in the hall said they can teach us to give an infant massage," April said now. "Let's set that up."

"Fine," I said absently, still deflated by the doctor's visit that afternoon. April left and reappeared with Christie, an occupational therapist eager to teach us the technique the nurses knew. Unzipping a bag in her hand, she moved to the table by my bed and set out bottles of lotions and oils.

"You mind taking off Annabelle's clothes?" she said. The energy in her voice was its own pain reliever, and the room filled with the sense of mercy I'd craved. I removed Annabelle's blanket and onesie, and we laid her on me, tummy down. April and Jonas sat on the couch behind where Christie stood.

"You two come help so I can teach you all," Christie said. My family team moved to the side of the bed opposite her. "Let's start with a prayer," she said. "Everyone place a hand on Annabelle."

Ahh, this was good. God was in charge, and Christie spoke our language. As she prayed and we all touched Annabelle's soft skin, we felt the Holy Spirit with us. I released a deep breath, and I felt my muscles unclench. Who knew lying in bed all day could knot a person like macramé? Holding a small container of lavender oil, Christie motioned for each of us to receive a dab.

"Everyone rub your hands together and take in the smell and feel," she directed. "Each of us will slowly massage one of Annabelle's limbs." Our girl's tiny arms had migrated up next to her head. Tenderly, I straightened and massaged them, shoulders to fingers. April and Jonas each took a pencil-sized leg, and Christie caressed her back. Annabelle released a sigh ending in a soft coo.

"This stimulates her central nervous system. It may help with her apnea or even avoid it," Christie explained. "It helps her produce more serotonin and stabilizes her heart rate and breathing."

Like Shelley, Christie led with compassion and care. To these medical personnel, our daughter was a real person, alive and breathing. Where others wore sad faces to grieve her limitations and my devotion to her, where others framed her existence in terms of death, Shelley and Christie unapologetically addressed her life. Entering a room, they could recharge the very ions in the air.

Annabelle dozed as we finished her massage, and then Christie left us with a kit of oils and new hope. That night Shelley came back, standing close to caress Annabelle's soft little scalp. We told her about the exit doctor and the massage. When Shelley offered to take Annabelle to the NICU to let Jonas and me sleep, I thought she was kidding. Then I weighed my trust in her with the zombie state Jonas and I had reached, and with the absence of medical personnel in our lives after today.

"You'll watch her like a hawk," I said. I sounded like a jeweler signing out a three-hour rental of the Hope Diamond. "If she has any issue, *anything*, you'll bring her immediately, even if I'm asleep."

Shelley frowned to match my scowl. "She will not leave my sight," she said seriously. "The NICU is slow tonight. Several of us will be on the job." I saw Jonas slump his agreement. Like mine, his eyes had become dark smudges. "I'll take her for three hours, and we can feed her when I return," Shelley said.

Two minutes later, maybe one, Annabelle's parents were fast asleep.

DAY FIVE

JANUARY 2

———————

O N CHECKOUT DAY, day five, we woke up rested. Following her first feeding, Annabelle had her longest apnea episode yet, our reminder that home would be a tightrope with no net. Both Jonas's and my employers had changed insurance companies effective January 1, multiplying our policies and everyone's paperwork. Hospital personnel moved in and out with discharge forms that might have been in Russian, given my ability that morning to comprehend or consider them.

Jonas was packing a final doll-sized diaper when Annabelle's apnea hit again. For one of the last times, we pressed a nearby button. A nurse sprinted in, and we massaged Annabelle until she gasped deeply, and the rest of us could return to our own regular breathing.

"I know we're supposed to check out now, but we can't," I said to the nurse pleadingly. "Could we possibly stay a little longer?"

The nurse gained permission to give us one hour more, two tops. The busy floor had to turn over our room, and in my arms Annabelle absorbed my anguish. Jonas and April bagged the rest of our belongings, set vases in boxes, collected medical supplies we'd been given, and then the clock said two o'clock, and I had wrung every last minute from our stay. Outside, the January day was cold and rainy. April and a nurse had helped me from the bed to a wheelchair. Downstairs, Jonas pulled our car to a door in a parking garage, and a newborn whose days no one knew to plan for was headed home. A doctor's note allowed me to sit in the back seat and hold her.

"You ready?" Jonas said, putting me in.

"Ready or not."

My chauffeur avoided the highway and eased over speed bumps, turning a fifteen-minute drive into half an hour. April's car, full of more items from our hospital stay, followed at a crawl. We pulled into our driveway in East Dallas, and it struck me that this was where Annabelle would leave us. The front door blew open, and Cameron was outside the car, arms wide. "ANNABELLE IS HOME!" he shouted, his cold over in time to host his sister's welcome. Jonas scooped Cameron into his arms to divert the exuberance.

"Hey, buddy!" he shouted, tossing a happy boy heavenward. "We missed you so much! How ya feeling today?"

"I'm great!" he said breathlessly. "I told you God would let Annabelle stay with us!"

Emerging from the back seat with our tiny bundle, I mentally replayed scenes here during my pregnancy. Now we were here together, Cameron chattering about his prayers to God. I looked at our sweet girl, breathing steadily in my arms. How often I'd lacked the faith to believe in this moment. How often I'd asked for God's will instead of asking for her to live because I feared my prayers would go unanswered. Inside, a homemade welcome banner draped across the fireplace mantle. Every surface sprouted with flowers and cards. Counters, floors, blinds, tables . . . were immaculate, the work of family and friends for Annabelle's safety. I hadn't realized how much I needed to be here.

Familiar sounds told me Jonas was in the kitchen making

dinner. I set up a portable crib and a woven baby carrier in our bedroom, then I changed little Annabelle into a fresh outfit and knit hat. The four of us sat together at the kitchen table that night—our first family meal at home—laughing at Cameron's accounts of the good life with his grandparents. Each gleeful story featured pauses to engage his sister.

"Annabelle, did you hear that? Your Farmor makes cookies really good! You can have one when you grow up a little!"

Jonas set out dessert, and we sang *Happy Birthday* to Annabelle, a daily ritual now because every day with her was another milestone. I handed her to her dad and led Cameron to his room to renew our nighttime routine of a book and prayers and snuggles. For the first time since my triple-extra-large stomach had gone down, I could hold him close.

"Cameron, you want to pray?" I said, dimming the lights.

"Dear God," he began, "thank you for my family and especially for my baby sister, Annabelle. I pray that everyone sleeps all through the night and we can do fun things tomorrow. I love her so much. Amen."

"Thank you, sweet angel," I said. "I'm glad you prayed hard for us to bring Annabelle home. I know God listened to you."

"He listens when I pray," Cameron said earnestly. I kissed Annabelle's brother on the cheek and tucked him into his toddler bed. Then I tiptoed into the living room where Jonas sat holding her.

"What's wrong?"

"She just stopped breathing for a second."

I lifted Annabelle from him to lie with her on my chest in a bedroom with no call button and no nurses nearby. Her heart grew more stable, but her breathing stayed rough, sending us into a long night. Jonas and I relieved each other. One of us would doze, and the other would jar awake. At times I was delirious, disoriented, more frightened than I'd expected.

DAY SIX

JANUARY 3

———————

W AKING UP TO day six was like crawling out of a train wreck. I felt hungover, physically sore, disoriented. Emotionally I felt newly orphaned, longing for the security of the medical experts gone from our lives. At nine o'clock that morning the doorbell rang, and Jonas got up. In minutes he was back.

"Who was it?" I said.

"It's April. She's here with a photographer."

"A *what*?"

"A friend of hers offered to do a photo shoot for us."

From the dresser mirror, a swollen face scowled at me. "I'm sorry, but no," I said.

"I don't like it either, Tricia, but they're here."

I could roll my eyes, or I could use them to sob. I dug through my closet and drawers for something that said post-pregnancy and yet was still huge. Out came a pair of maternity jeans with a grey-and-white striped sweater. I moved into the bathroom for high-level damage control. From there I grudgingly entered our living room, parts of it shoved aside and stacked to clear space for a photo shoot. April held Annabelle as she discussed lighting with the photographer.

"Good morning!" my sister said to me cheerily, and I looked at her. "What's wrong?" she said.

What's wrong? My eyes swept in the room and stopped at Annabelle in her arms. "We have nothing left in us, and I don't want to do this," I said faintly.

"I know you don't, but you'll thank me."

Maybe. April had the family thing going for her. For six months I'd let a film crew shadow almost every aspect of our life. I would survive one more shoot. However invasive, it could also capture fleeting moments in a short life, an issue of urgency April knew to seize even when I couldn't. Within half an hour, I knew something exceptional was afoot. Annabelle was awake, for one thing, and Cameron was cooperating, always evidence of a miracle. Then during a break for another setup Cameron asked me if he could hold Annabelle, and the rest of the room waited for my answer.

He was always so sweet with her. "Sure, buddy, we can do that," I said. Cameron climbed into a blue wingback chair and faced me, hands outstretched.

"I'll be careful with her," he promised, and I believed him. As gently as committing a jewel to its setting, I lowered a new little sister into her brother's arms.

"Watch her head, buddy. You have to support it because she can't control it herself."

"Like this?" His right arm moved higher and behind her head.

"Just like that."

Then Cameron was in his world, singing to his sister. April nudged me and stealthily raised her camera. "I looooove Annabelle," he was singing in a narrative with a few holes. "One day, I woke up and there was a baby in mommy's tummy, and I thought that it was Annabelle, but it waaaaaasn't. It was Annabelle, and she came out! I loooove Annabelle!" Warming to his lyrics, he raised the volume, and we watched in wonder.

By the time the shoot wrapped, a grateful mother was happy to eat her words. I thanked April the Organizer and the generous photographers and headed to my bedroom to join an overdue family nap. Annabelle had stayed awake for photos and was crashing. We'd purchased the alarm for the front of her diaper, and I laid her in her playpen so Jonas and I could pass out next to her. Cameron fell asleep in his room. And in what surely was the next moment, like an air-raid siren sounding next to our ears, a shrill blast tore into our nerves.

Jonas materialized at Annabelle's side. "Give her to me! Put her on my chest!" I shouted. I peeled back my shirt, and he laid her face down. Limb by limb we massaged as aggressively as we dared. Maybe thirty seconds later, maybe hours, her chest rose and fell again, and I wiped tears from under my chin. So close. So close. And each time the fear undid me.

> We couldn't keep her, we knew that. But she was ours, and our goodbye would be final, and we dreaded it.

Annabelle was not a statistic or a groundbreaking case for the next medical conference. She was our daughter, with our features and coloring, and a brother, and grandparents, and a community of people who loved and wanted her. For nine months I carried her, and I gave birth to her. We were not philosophic about her short life or detached from her pain. We fought to have her, fought to know and love her, fought for time with her. For her part, she broke every notion of what doctors said was possible. We couldn't keep her, we knew that. But she was ours, and our goodbye would be final, and we dreaded it.

When the apnea episode subsided, instead of trying to go back to sleep, someone suggested we give her a bath to calm us all. Jonas found a small-ish container that had made it home from the hospital, and he filled it with warm water. I tested the temperature and eased her in, holding the back of her head. She relaxed into the warmth. Her eyes, big and blue, met ours as she went limp, trusting and placid. Dabbing baby shampoo on a miniature washcloth, we made her clean and comfortable. In her six days of life, she had shrunk from lack of nutrition. Gently we patted her dry and put her in fresh clothes. I desperately wanted food in her belly.

The hospital had insisted on no feeding tube, but my instincts told me now to push for one. If Annabelle had little time to live, why suffer with starvation? Again, what about that had to do with comfort? That night Jonas and I straightened the house and spent time reading to Cameron and holding him. Too soon we'd have to decide whether he should be with us when she passed. I'd think about it tomorrow. A person could handle only so much in one day, and we'd hit quota early.

In the night Annabelle had more small episodes. Around four in the morning her heart stopped and for more than a minute she lay inert. Jonas and I were holding each other and her, crying inconsolably, when she took a deep breath and her eyes reopened. With a few more gasps her breathing returned to a rhythm, and she slept again. I couldn't stop crying, and I couldn't put her down.

And I couldn't bear much more. We'd think she was gone, and my heart would break, and she'd revive, each episode causing her no pain but depleting us all.

"This is killing me. We have to get food into her," I said to Jonas, and he reminded me it was 4:15 a.m.

'We'll figure it out," he said. "We have to have some sleep."

"And in the morning, let's get Cameron to someone else's house."

"But if we don't sleep, we can't do anything."

DAY SEVEN

JANUARY 4

D AY SEVEN FOUND us groggy and emotionally drained. Jonas took Annabelle into the living room to be with Cameron and to give me a moment alone, but when I tried to sit up, C-section pain seared through me. The label on my pain meds said every four to six hours. Best I could recall, my last dosage was the day before yesterday.

I was supposed to walk in the house, drink glasses of water, and get real sleep. Instead my days went to crying, time in bed with Annabelle, and worrying myself into paralysis. During my pregnancy I'd skeptically learned deep-breathing exercises. Now, too low even for doubting, I took a deep breath, counted to ten, and exhaled. Then I repeated it. With each breath, tears coursed from me, taking tension with them. For long minutes, I inhaled, exhaled, and wept.

I thought of my pregnancy and of Annabelle's birth. Going back to early May of the year before, I replayed scene after scene and cried, and then I cried more. And then, like salt in the soup, in the grief I tasted gratitude. We'd come so far, done so much. A three-pound little girl with a two-chamber heart had lived for six days —six days longer than anyone expected. A single moment to see and hold her would have made it worthwhile, and we got more. We believed we'd see her again. We knew God was in control, and that he is good. We had no regrets. And then it hit me that I would regret finding no way to nourish her. Whatever time was left, with every apnea episode she survived, our daughter was dying for food.

Taking the shortest route to a solution, I called April. "We have to feed her," I said. "She needs a tube, and we have to figure out a way."

"You want me to post on Facebook for medical opinions?" April knew our doctors and nurses had always pushed back. "You sure that's what you want to do?"

"That's what we have to do," I said, and I waited for my sister's signature reply.

"I'll get on it," she said. "I'll let you know what I hear as soon as possible." We hung up, and for a moment I basked in my best first call. I prayed for April to find the right person and the right help. If we sat on a mountain of miracles, I reasoned, why not ask for another.

Buoyed by hope, I could get out of bed now and shower. Mourning would come, but sadness and anxiety would not steal from our time left with Annabelle, even as the apnea episodes made it difficult to push away the "what ifs." Drying off, I heard Jonas's parents in the living room, there to take Cameron for the day and the next night, which relieved me too. They left, and a few moments later April arrived.

"Good news!" she all but shouted. "A friend of mine will come this afternoon. She's a nurse. She has the supplies to try to put in a feeding tube for Annabelle." Just as I'd hoped. And just as quickly came the fears, and then my sense that we had to take the risk. The next hours brought more apnea—shorter episodes, less severe than the night before, but painful to witness—and my decision was made.

Early that afternoon a knock on the door brought in two nurses, both in scrubs, who followed April into the living room to meet with Jonas and me. "First," said Becky, the dark-haired nurse, "we do not represent where we work. We're here simply as friends to try to help Annabelle in any way." Becky was April's trusted friend.

The fair-haired nurse spoke: "We saw your post, and we think we can help."

"Next," Becky said, "we cannot guarantee if we give Annabelle a feeding tube that she will not aspirate. Regardless, we believe we should try." Her words went to my soul, and I agreed.

In the hospital I'd wondered whether doctors had refused Annabelle a feeding tube to avoid the blame if something went wrong. A label is a fearsome thing. The words Trisomy 18 too often cause medical personnel, I'm convinced, to see a child in terms of death instead of potential for life. The test that revealed Annabelle's condition at three months is hardly common. Most parents of Trisomy 18 children learn of it much further into the pregnancy or even after the child is born. If I hadn't known, what might my pregnancy and Annabelle's life have been? Regardless, here in our living room was our next miracle: two nurses willing to help us feed our child.

"Thank you for coming," I said. "Without milk she could be gone in hours." Empathy and respect showed on their faces. "Her passing is inevitable," I added, "but we have to do all we can."

"We're going to wash up now," Becky said. "Please lay out a blanket and take off her clothes so we can watch her chest and monitor her progress."

In the back and forth, I'd hardly let Jonas or April speak. "Are you both okay with this?" I asked them now. "We won't do this if you disagree."

"She's hungry and we need to feed her. I feel right about that," Jonas said. April nodded. The three of us moved into the master bedroom and stood around the bed. Jonas spread out a child's blanket. I laid Annabelle on it. We undressed her to her diaper and turned her onto her back.

"May we all pray first?" April asked. We held hands around Annabelle, leaned over the bed, and I was free of doubt. April prayed for the tube to go in well and for nutrients to strengthen Annabelle for the hours ahead. By the end of the prayer, I sensed the Holy Spirit's presence, and the nurses went to work. One inserted a tube while the other listened through a stethoscope to Annabelle's chest. Slowly the small transparent pipe disappeared into her nose. Slowly the part we could see grew shorter.

What surprised me was Annabelle's calm. "We're close," a nurse said, the stethoscope in her ears. Minutes later, the tube was in position to send milk into our child's stomach.

"Now to test it," Becky said, my cue to put a small quantity of my milk into a syringe and insert the syringe into the tube. Slowly my milk traveled toward her nose and then beyond. My sweaty palms slipped once, but I pressed again firmly to send it further down. Annabelle fidgeted, her body pushing left and right, her eyes alternately on Jonas and me. And then a new string of looks showed on her face: surprise, confusion . . . bliss. This beat sucking a Q-Tip, and the nurses continued to monitor.

"Am I doing it right?" I asked.

"You're perfect," one said. They both broke into smiles. The tube was in, and the milk was in Annabelle's stomach. For a moment we were out of the woods.

Annabelle had received a thimble of liquid with ease, and she began to sleep off her meal. Her breathing grew deep, and her face relaxed. Carefully, gently, the nurses taped the tube around her nose. Then they reviewed the steps with us for future feedings. I tried to take in their instructions, but something in Annabelle's relaxed state had triggered my own exhaustion. My eyes may have crossed, and then I glanced at April, busy taking notes on her phone.

Whatever happened next, our Florence Nightingales had helped us feed our daughter. Before leaving, they caressed the sleeping beauty. "Take care of yourselves," Becky said to Jonas and me. "You need your energy to take care of her."

"God bless you both," the second nurse said. "It's an honor to help your daughter."

For hours Annabelle slept more soundly than we'd ever seen. She awoke happy and content, taking us in with her big round eyes. All that afternoon we lived in her moment, relishing her awareness and peace, giving our anxieties a half day off. When we caressed her little head, she'd turn toward us for more. Despite a few short apnea bouts, we could see the nutrients' effects. That evening, Jonas, April, and I took turns napping and holding Annabelle in our human chain of love.

Late that evening the alarm on her diaper went off. We massaged vigorously and watched. Eventually she moved again, and then we could too, but the strain stayed in her face and breathing. We decided to go back to sleep and trust the alarm to wake us.

If you've ever tried to sleep near train tracks, the whistle of the approaching train more than awakens you, it explodes in you down to your cellular level. The device on Annabelle's diaper was that abrasive, but in our lives it had a high purpose. For however long our battle lasted, when the call came for Annabelle to leave us, I would be with her.

DAY EIGHT

JANUARY 5

———————

A LITTLE AFTER MIDNIGHT the alarm exploded, sending us to our posts like medics on call. Jonas and April massaged Annabelle's little limbs while I held her to my chest and whispered in her ear. "It's okay. You can do it. Just breathe, baby girl. I love you so much."

But her limbs yielded too softly this time. Her eyelids drooped and not in relief. Her beautiful color drained. Day by day, every episode had prepared us for the next, but every episode drained her, and nothing prepares a mother to see her child give up. Time slowed, and then it stopped. Our Annabelle lay limp, and my mind told me this was it. We waited until there was no more waiting, and then Jonas and April and I prayed over the little object of our intense love. We thanked God for her life, crowded with meaning, and I tried to absorb the finality of what I'd worked so hard to keep at bay.

I wrapped our little girl in a blanket and cradled her. For so much of Annabelle's short life, I had felt her more than seen her. Now I stared into her eyes. I rocked her, clinging to the moments before I'd have to think and act again. Jonas called the number he'd been given if our daughter died at home. The paperwork for her eventual passing had sat in our kitchen untouched, impossible to read when we had her, impossible to read now.

"He'll be here within the hour," Jonas said. I thought about the man receiving a father's sad call. I thought about his work answering death in the night. Annabelle had come five minutes into the new day. She'd lived 150 hours. From 8:10 p.m. on December 29 to 12:05 a.m. on January 5, we'd shared her lifetime, joy to grief. Back and forth I rocked her, back and forth. Forty-five minutes after Jonas's call, a light knock sounded at the front door. I could hear whispering, then Jonas and a stranger crossed the living room to where I sat in the kitchen with Annabelle.

He was an older man with a briefcase. "I'm sorry for your loss, Mrs. Roos. She's a beautiful baby," he said. He seemed sad too. He asked Jonas about Annabelle's death and about our past few hours. I strained to memorize the curves in her delicate face and button nose, the perfect orb of her head, her soft hair, the sweet smell of her clothes and blanket.

"I'll need to take her now, ma'am," the man was saying, and I thought I complied, but when I looked, she was still with me. Jonas pressed my shoulder. "It's okay. We need to give Annabelle to him," he said, and the man had our daughter.

"Is there a bed where I can lay her down to put this over her?" he asked. On his left arm was a child's blanket. I led him to our room and cleared a place on the bed. Carefully he laid our daughter down. Carefully he spread out the large white cloth and placed her little body at its center. Each corner he folded across her and tucked in until all of our Annabelle was covered, and I collapsed on the floor.

Death should look like old age, like the grandparents my family had buried at the ends of their long lives. Annabelle should be in a room with toys and books and clothes, covered with kisses instead of a stranger's blanket. When the man walked to the door, Jonas held me from behind. In what was left of the night, at some point we slept or passed out.

The next morning a knock on the door woke me and for a

fraction of a second I believed Annabelle was next to our bed, sleeping, and I looked in the basket and saw a folded blanket. The clock on the dresser said 9:30, easily the latest I'd slept since college days, and now I could hear my father's voice. He must have waited for hours before making the twenty-minute drive from North Dallas. I walked into the living room and fell into his arms.

"She's no longer suffering,' he said. "She's in a better place" — and I blazed inside at the phrases that would loop endlessly through our next weeks and months. People could keep their condolences. I wanted Annabelle, not sympathy. I wanted more time with our daughter. More time. I wasn't sad, I was angry— and everything I'd been told about grief was a lie. What about the pain that guts your insides? What about the sense of injustice? People came to our house. They left notes or food. They stayed, they talked, they left. I wanted Annabelle. April posted the news on "Annabelle's Army," but I didn't want support. I wanted what was taken from me. For all of the clarity I'd had about her birth, Annabelle was gone, and the emptiness brought only darkness.

> People could keep their condolences. I wanted Annabelle, not sympathy.

The next morning Cameron burst through the front door, home from Farmor's, darting room to room. "Annabelle!" he shouted. "Where are you hiding, little sister?" He giggled and looked through closets and the laundry room.

"Cameron," I said from the bedroom, "come see me so we can talk." He ran in looking perplexed.

"Where's Annabelle, Mommy?"

I tried to pull him into my lap, but he was still on the hunt. "That's what I wanted to talk to you about, sweetheart," I said, reaching to stroke his hair. "Do you remember we said when I was pregnant that Annabelle might have to go back to heaven so God can make her healthy?"

"Yes," he said, his little head cocked, "but God gave her to us and we got to keep her."

"It's true. And we got to take her home, and that was wonderful. But last night God took Annabelle back home to heaven, and now she's with him." Saying the words, I began to shake, and Cameron began to cry. Jonas came in and left with Cameron in his arms.

For the next week Jonas, Cameron, April, and I kept mostly to ourselves. People had no idea what to say to us, and we had nothing to say. And there was the funeral—no, the celebration of life—to think about. Outside of Cameron, no one had believed Annabelle could live one minute. Yet for a week and a lifetime, with her little two-chamber heart and her beautiful coloring, she had breathed and slept and responded. And we loved her. And that we would celebrate.

In planning the service, the frigid winter in me showed the first signs of spring. Whatever the pain, we'd had a chance to get to know her. I thought often of the dream during my pregnancy, the vivid scene of a full house at our church, everyone singing and praising God. That morning I'd woken knowing her arrival and departure were perfectly timed. It's hard to sustain the moments of certainty, but we can return to them, and in them the sadness and anger lose some of their edge. Annabelle's celebration service would be no day in the park, but there were things to say, and the dream framed my thinking.

Several times during my pregnancy, certain songs had sustained Jonas and me. Now I wanted them in Annabelle's service. My volleyball manager, a leader in the Bishop Lynch choir, had a beautiful voice. He would sing several of the pieces. Another volleyball resource, a top player and talented videographer, offered to make a montage to celebrate Annabelle. Thousands of people had prayed for her and prayed for us, but precious few had met her, and we gratefully accepted.

Public speaking was second nature to me but not at my child's funeral, and we handed that to April. The service grew closer, and I was angry and sad and grateful, and at times I was strangely joyful.

A DREAM COME TRUE

———

THE WORST FUNERALS are the ones for children. People in the pews stare at the mother hoping they never have to know what she knows, and now I was that mother. One part of me wanted the day behind us, another part of me needed to shout from the rooftops that our beautiful daughter had defied every expert's opinion, every prediction, to live for a week and change us forever.

Then again, what if no one came? What if our massive church echoed with the emptiness inside us now? What if my grief took over and I made a wreck of the day? The service announcement told people to wear bright colors, but until that morning I'd given no thought to what I would wear. When I looked through my closet, no dress that fit my body fit the occasion, and I wept for every hurt and disappointment in the past ten months and for this crowning day of more than I thought I could endure. A final hopeless search surfaced a bright red dress—redemptive red, I thought—and this close to Christmas, I could still wear it.

The three o'clock service was timed to allow Bishop Lynch to let out early for any students, faculty or staff wanting to come, making for a long day for us. An hour after lunch, Jonas, Cameron and I grew restless, drove to the church, and went to the room set up for our family and lead pastor. Someone there reviewed the service format with me. About a half hour before, I could hear people coming into the sanctuary, and I peered through a crack in the side door. At the front of the church, between sprays of pink flowers, sat an oversized portrait of Annabelle taken by April's photographer. Hundreds of familiar faces filled pews, and as trivial as it sounds, I was relieved. A piano started to play, and I turned back into the room.

The minute hand on the big wall clock jerked silently to the number three. Jonas and I joined the pastor at the door, and our parents and siblings fell in line behind us. I'd seen entire families walk the length of the sanctuary to begin and end a funeral service, but that was out of the question. From the front right of the sanctuary we filed into a first-row pew, and I turned to look behind us. In ten minutes, the crowd had doubled into the scene from my dream. The lights, the music, the people—months before I'd previewed this with a trusted childhood guide. Now the large hole in me filled with faith, and I knew God was there.

The music started, and Alvin's clear tenor rose above the sea of voices. Like the tail of a comet in the night sky, the sound soared and faded. I sang loudly and through tears, suspended in harmony beyond music. On the pew between Jonas and me, I could hear Cameron's sweet voice. How much he understood, I was unsure. I wrapped my arms around him and reached for Jonas.

Eventually the congregation sat, and our pastors spoke—Jeff and Sam, our supporters through the months—giving voice to the faith that had held us when our own grasps grew slack. Though Jonas and I only recently had joined a new Sunday school class, its members seemed to be everywhere, greeting, volunteering, supplying and serving the food at the reception. Pastor Jeff spoke from Psalm 139:13, where the songwriter says God knew him before his mother saw him. Before Annabelle was created, God knew her life would matter. He had crafted her in my womb. Her life was not random, and the assurance calmed me.

Then April stepped up to the impossible task of thanking people for us and to give a picture of Annabelle's brief life. "You showed up at the hospital, at our doorsteps, and through phone calls and email," she said to the crowd. "Some of you came and prayed over us, and we never even knew you were there."

She recounted a scene I loved of her conversation with Cameron at the start of his campaign for a lady baby. "I've asked God every day, sometimes twice a day, and we still don't have one," he'd said to April. "Mommy and I have tried everything!" April described the pregnancy, the test that turned our world upside down, the months of pain always inseparable from blessings. She listed the miracles of Annabelle's beauty, "those pink cheeks medically impossible with her two-chamber heart," her nose like her big brother's, her response to his voice, the feeding tube, the 150 hours of a life that no expert would have given thirty minutes.

"And what happened in our lives because of Annabelle is what God desires for all us," April said. "He wants us to know him, and love him, and draw near to him, and depend on him. St. Augustine said, 'You have made us for yourself, O Lord, and our hearts are restless until they find their rest in you.'"

April ended with the hope that sustained me. "Annabelle Marie Roos, you were a lot of fun, baby girl, and we miss you," she said, "but we will see you again, soon, on a day far better and brighter than this." She stepped away, and a video montage ran pictures from the hospital and in our home. As with so many things concerning Annabelle, the service was wrenching and therapeutic and full of "more than here, more than now." Afterwards in a large drawing room downstairs, where our Sunday school class had set up desserts and drinks, Jonas, Cameron and I took our places at the entrance to greet people.

"You okay?" Jonas asked me, and in a sense I was because the dream seemed everywhere around us. Down the corridor, I saw a line form with no visible end, holding every person in our lives for the past decade. "I can do this," I said. I fell into a rhythm of "thank you," "thank you for coming," "thank you for your condolences," until Shelley and the nursing staff from Baylor reached the front of the line.

I'd wondered if anyone from the hospital would be there. NICU nurses live by tight schedules, and they can hardly mourn every child that dies. But they'd come and waited in the long line, and my heart turned to them the way little Annabelle's head turned to Cameron's voice. Here was Shelley, my hope when all seemed lost, and the women who knew and loved Annabelle, and we wept and embraced like sisters.

WISH AGAIN

EVERY ENDING IS A BEGINNING

NO ONE BUYS a movie ticket to see the bad guy get the girl or the underdog stay down, but real-life happy endings are more complex. Which is to say the close to Annabelle's story is still a work in progress.

On her birthdays I mourn as if she died yesterday. But even painful endings also invite new beginnings, and we got one of those too. After a full-term pregnancy, women generally are told to wait at least eighteen months to have another child. Six months after Annabelle's death, however—and two short months after emergency gallbladder surgery—I was pregnant with Andie, back in the now-surreal cycle of milestones and doctors' visits.

More than a year before, when my doctor's office called with results from my cfDNA test, I'd expected a technician to give me gender news. That time, Dr. Martin was on the line and my world imploded. After the second test, my only concern was chromosomes. When Dr. M called, I answered with, "Please give me good news." This time she laughed and said she was giving me permission for a small glass of pink champagne to salute our healthy girl. Healthy, she said. Healthy. A few days later my friends and I began planning the baby showers I'd turned down for Annabelle.

Still, those months were up and down. When I was happy it felt as if I was cheating on Annabelle. When I was sad it felt unfair to Andie. A day finally came when my two daughters shared a single field of light. Jonas and I planned for two children and got three. Losing Annabelle had led to Andie—our sun after the storm, our rainbow of personality with unruly blonde curls serving anyone as ample warning. As for Cameron, no matter their five-year age difference (such an issue with women having kids), Andie cuddles next to him on the couch. She looks up to him. When they're not locking horns, he takes care of her.

Let the world define a good life as a long one. Not that early death doesn't hurt—our minds go to the unlived potential and years—but in God's economy "brief" comes with mystery. You don't get over the loss, but you survive it. And between what was and what will be, you love all your children. I have a friend who lost her three-year-old daughter in a tragic accident and recently gave birth to her fourth child. Almost daily she still posts a picture of her daughter on Facebook. A parent who loses a child knows the compulsion to memorialize, to press purpose out of tragedy.

For months after Annabelle's death, I shunned anyone I didn't know. *Just give me people who loved my daughter*, I thought. Then one day I told someone new that one of our children had defied the experts and lived a lifetime in six days. And I said it without crying. Not long after that, talking to a total stranger, I found myself smiling over a story about Annabelle. Something important was shifting.

How often do I think about her? Every day. And not morbidly, not at all. It's like the sick man in the Bible whose friends lowered him through a roof to Jesus. After Jesus forgave his sins and healed him, he told the man to roll up his mat and take it with him. Think about that. That mat stood for everything the man hated—his sickness, his discomfort, his non-normal life, his weakness and need—everything he'd want to leave behind. But as a preacher pointed out, the mat wasn't carrying the man anymore, he was carrying it.

Certain people learn the paradox of growing stronger as they carry the past. At first, every thought is a gut punch. Eventually you smile at a memory without feeling disloyal, and you think of your child without sadness. Annabelle stays in our nightly family prayers, and I found an answer to the frequent question about how many children we have. We have three. Not two living and one gone, but two on earth and one in heaven. After that, it's easy to say more—though I may glance away or down because I don't want the other person's pity. I'm happy, and I know Annabelle is.

Is she forever a baby to us? I've been asked that. We knew her as a newborn, and pictures of her at home and at work evoke that sweet baby smell and her soft noises. But I'll see a little girl about her age now and try to imagine who she'd be. She'd be stubborn like me. She'd smile and laugh on a dime. If I try to conjure her voice or look, I hit a wall and the dreamer in me sags, and it's all right. Annabelle wasn't expected to live at all, and the effects of her short life go on.

Get Help

A person can read about loss, study it, see others suffer . . . and then it hits home, and it's a blindside. In the days right after Annabelle's death, just getting out of bed was a long-range goal. Even now, something will happen, and I'll have to reframe my thinking of her in terms of hope and not despair. So when people ask me what to say to others in grief, my answer is *very little*. Grief has stages, but as far as I know it has no shortcuts or magic words.

Most grieving parents want to cherish their memories, not erase them. Talk to them about the child. Let them know their son or daughter matters to you too. As time passes, you might set a reminder to call, text or email every two or three months to say you're thinking about them. On a birthday, send balloons, flowers or a card. If it sounds unkind to stir up parents' dormant memories, believe me, their memories are not dormant.

What you don't want to do is compare their loss to anything. Losing a child is not like losing your grandpa or your dog or your best friend. The words "ministry of presence" reminds us to just be. Just show up and, unless you're a grief counselor, however awkward it may be for you, lie low on the advice.

Community

To try to survive tragedy without help is a setup for another tragedy. Don't do that yourself, and don't let anyone else. Annabelle's story was news, and a lot of people were aware of our ordeal. We weren't alone. Not every loss requires a Facebook page to keep people current, but every loss requires other people. If you're suffering, let your friends know, and let them help. Annabelle came home to a house cleaned and sanitized by people who loved her because they loved us, and we said thank you. When I couldn't think straight, I could lean on longstanding relationships.

Society hard sells us on social networks for power and connection, but the more we depend on social media the weaker our true lifelines. I'm big on using my phone to have a conversation and stay in touch. For the relationships that sustain my life, and my family's lives, if I can't see our people in person, my phone lines stay warm.

Also, relationships are two-way doors. Like the call to Peggy Wehmeyer, when I reach an obstacle or challenge, I find someone whose insight can improve my perspective, and I do the same for others. After my cfDNA test results, I went to *many* mothers of Trisomy 18 children. Now I talk to women beginning the journey I know. And in the give and take of our weaknesses and strengths, pains and needs, God's grace thrives.

Face the Healing

When Annabelle died, I cried for days on end, and when I finally looked up, I was lost. My C-section qualified me for an eight-week maternity leave, and the school gives bereavement time, but maternity leave without a baby felt wrong. And too much solitude is its own black hole. One day I showed up at school and dove into the busiest part of the admissions season. Then summer volleyball came, and by July I was pregnant again.

But the grief we shove out of our days comes roaring back on its own schedule, and sometime in winter 2017-'18, anxiety and depression laid me flat. And did I see a therapist? Not once. Because no one in our insurance looked like a fit, and because $100-plus an hour seemed like my cue to solve my own problems. Not until five years after Annabelle's death did I see a church grief counselor who charged no fee—a friend connected us. Every session left me pounds lighter and five rough years wiser.

If you've had a loss and think you powered through it, my advice is to run, don't walk, for professional wisdom. And when you get it, slow down for the process. Grief isn't a box to check or an obstacle to clear. All the talk about the stages—shock, anger, denial, depression—are true. They may lessen as we go, but they recycle, and like anything else, we need to know what's happening.

Going Forward

In families, men and women tend to grieve differently. Within those broad categories, we have our own styles. I'm a crier, for instance. Jonas is a protector, forever putting his family first. The more I grieved, the more he pushed down his own grief to attend to my pregnancy, birth, and hospital stay, and to Annabelle's death and funeral.

Jonas and I never sought counseling during my pregnancy or after Annabelle's death. In hindsight, a seasoned therapist might have helped us more wisely navigate the rough waters and know what grief is. What it's not, for instance, is a score card about who grieves more openly. Good grief allows for every person's expression and pace. Good grief has priorities. Family, friends and community are essential, but our marriage, our partnership, is paramount. No one else can know the depths of our pain or experience. Annabelle was *our* flesh and blood. *We* created her.

Cameron is shot through with the tenderness that Annabelle brought out in all of us, and I'm grateful for it. Parents who try to protect older siblings from a brush with death, even using it as a reason to terminate a pregnancy, tend to shortchange everyone. To involve the siblings, to respect their places in the love and the grief, is work for the parents. But the siblings who know they belong even in a family's hard times gain important life tools.

I'm a believer now in outside help. At the start of the Covid-19 pandemic, in the endless reports of people dying from an illness doctors couldn't fix, we had Cameron talk to a counselor. In the next months we saw tremendous improvement in how he handled the fear in the air, the absence of playmates, the adult frenzy to avoid a menace no one could see. Did Annabelle's death intensify his emotions? Sure. But whether or not he becomes the doctor who cures Trisomy 18, as he sometimes says, her life will have a tremendous impact on his future, and in a good way.

As for Andie, she tells anyone who will listen that she has a big sister in heaven. She speaks naturally of her older sister and asks about her. When we look at photos in our house of a baby girl, she'll say, "Is that Annabelle, Mommy, or is that baby Andie?" She'll want to hear the same stories over and over. Andie knows she belongs to a family with one foot already in heaven.

Annabelle's life continues to help me depend on a God I cannot see and a plan I can never script for myself. I'm still a Type A—I don't see that changing—and I still struggle with events I can't control. I learned to trust God with Annabelle, but I can still have difficulty trusting others. I've known depression and anxiety, but I love my life and where I fit in the world.

The Faith Factor

A family's flesh-and-blood loss can overwhelm its confidence in the God they can't see. "In our grief we cried out to God and got the wrong answer," they say. "He must have abandoned us," and it's easy to descend into bitterness. I cried out to God, but seldom in anger, I think, because in his mercy he gave me some sense that the pain had a purpose, and that my part was to trust. Nothing shielded me from the hard days, mentally or physically, or from the loss or the depression, but I also knew something else was at work.

God reveals himself to all of us every day. If we're open to him, our faith can grow and so can our resilience in his purpose. Like the prodigal son, when we start down the road to him—in any sense of starting down the road—he's running down to meet us, robes flying. That's the picture Jesus gives. As soon as I say it, I also have to say that my faith still wavers. I still go through periods of pain and have to stop and hit reset. When I do—when I recognize my weaknesses and confess my sins—God is faithful and sees to it that none of the pain is wasted.

We're in this world to learn to love. What I know is that suffering is a teacher, which sounds like terrible psychology, but it really is a profound truth. Like childbirth, what we gain redeems the pain. Like childbirth, and like Jesus going to his death, we don't want to avoid it or somehow detach from it, but get through it. Even as Jesus suffered, he transformed the pain with love. From the cross, he asked God to forgive the people who put him there. In our moments of weakness, the physical world becomes a key to the spiritual world.

It makes sense if you accept a few basic premises, like the rules in volleyball. If you accept that God exists and is good, and that you can know him, that's a lot to build on. Almost every other religion says to let go of the physical world to be free to get to the spiritual world. Christianity says what comes to us in the physical world leads to eternity. A lot of things about faith, like prayer, we do before we understand it or its ultimate effects. In love and obedience, we form certain habits—and at different markers we see ways that our habits are forming us.

I still think of the Christmas service at Bishop Lynch just before my pregnancy. It was about Mary at Jesus's birth—her pure heart, her saying yes to God in her trouble and sorrow. She teaches us to take suffering and hand it back to God, and what he ultimately puts in our hands, if we'll let him, is more than we could ever have wished for.

ACKNOWLEDGEMENTS

To Jonas, my husband, your strength in my life shines out in these pages. Thank you for supporting the idea of *When Wishes Change* and for waiting until I got near the end to read it and comment. To the family I love as friends and the friends who step up like family, if you don't see yourself here or feel the gratitude, just read between the lines. To my co-workers, and to my church family and pastors: By name or by implication, you're in every chapter, too, and thank you. For the doctors and nurses in the business of giving life in spirit as well as in deed, there are no words. To my editor, Nancy Lovell, who's all about words, here's to teamwork.

Getting this story into a book was often difficult, frequently a relief, at times fun, almost always therapeutic. The big help was knowing that I was supposed to tell it. The same hope that got me through my daughter's life and death got me through the hard chapters because I knew—*I know*—that all of this belongs to a plan too big for me to make out.

Finally, this book is not even printed and already it's bursting my borders—saying to not just Trisomy 18 parents but to *anyone* that no tragedy has the last word. God's love has the last word. *When Wishes Change* is here to remind you, down to your marrow, that even if you never fully understand a hard thing that happens to you, God means it for your good. And that changes everything.

LEARN. SHARE. GROW.

BECAUSE OUR STORIES GO ON

For behind-the-scenes photos and videos of the Roos family and footage of her team's state championship, go to:

TriciaRoos.com
(To have Tricia at your next event, click on "speaker.")

Facebook: Facebook.com/whenwisheschange

Instagram: @whenwisheschange

TikTok: @whenwisheschange

LinkedIn: Tricia Roos

Printed in the United States
by Baker & Taylor Publisher Services